HOW TO BE A FREELA

In this Series

Other titles in preparation

BE A FREELANCE JOURNALIST

Your step-by-step guide to success

Christine Hall

How To Books

British Library Cataloguing in Publication Data
A catalogue record for this book is available from the British Library.

First published in 1995 by How To Books Ltd, Plymbridge House, Estover Road, Plymouth PL6 7PZ, United Kingdom. Tel: Plymouth (01752) 735251/ 695745. Fax: (01752) 695699. Telex: 45635.

Note: The material contained in this book is set out in good faith for general guidance and no liability can be accepted for loss or expense incurred as a result of relying in particular circumstances on statements made in the book. The law and regulations are complex and liable to change, and readers should check the current position with the relevant authorities before making personal arrangements.

Typeset by Concept Communications (Design & Print) Ltd, Crayford, Kent. Printed and bound by The Cromwell Press, Broughton Gifford, Melksham, Wiltshire.

Contents

List of Illustrations

Foreword

This is a book that tells you 'everything you want to know but never dared to ask' about beginning and maintaining a career as a freelance journalist.

Christine Hall knows the business from both sides: she has been a journalist and an editor. As well as showing you how to write and present your work for the various markets, she knows what editors want and she passes on this valuable information to her readers. (Many of the chapters include a What The Editors Say section.)

Christine also takes the would-be journalist behind the scenes into the office of a magazine, showing you step by step what becomes of your manuscript after you have posted it. (Not a chapter for the faint-hearted, but immensely useful for serious writers.)

This book is almost a writing course in itself, with checklists of things to do at every stage of your work, reading lists, sample letters, and sections on photography, marketing and payment.

There is, though, one thing no publication can give you: an exchange of ideas. For this you need to join a writers' group or organisation. (See Chapters 1 and 12.) Don't be intimidated by the thought that people you will meet are 'published' writers and you are not. Arm yourself with Christine's book — *read every chapter, don't skip anything; above all, don't give up* — and you soon will be.

Mary Rensten
Chair, Society of Women Writers and Journalists 1992-1995

Preface

Over 10,000 magazines and newspapers are published in the UK alone. This means there is a huge market for freelance writing, especially for features and articles.

Freelance journalism is a competitive field; but it is accessible to everyone. With hard work, determination, and the knowledge of what editors really want it is possible to earn good income from freelance writing. This book shows how to succeed.

Special thanks to everyone who helped with this book: writers Claire Gill, Diana Lloyd Taylor, Mary Victoria Webb, Lynda Rajan and Norman Toulson for proofreading and criticising the manuscript; journalists Jane Baker, John Dawes and Mike Gerrard for the interviews in Chapter 13; writers Evelyn Thomsen, Jill Dick, Mary Rensten, Molly Perham and Rosemary Wells for their encouragement and advice; editors (feature editors, editorial assistants) Martin Oxley of *The Kent & Sussex Courier*, Mary Bryce of *Chat,* Suzanne Riley of *Quartos*, Charlotte Collis of *Popular Crafts Magazine*, Diana K Jones of *The Disabled Driver*, Gail Robinson of *What Personal Computer*, Ian Boughton of *Stationery Trade News*, Jane Simon of *Woman*, Steve Windsor of *Practical Fishkeeping*, Erika Harvey of *Here's Health*, John T Wilson of *Great Ideas*, Helene Hodge of *Active Life*, Michael Furnall of *Stamp Lover*, Kathryn Joyce of *PC Magazine*, Peter Merring of *Steam Classic*, Brian Attwood of *The Stage and Television Today*, Alan Travell of *Freelance Writing & Photography* and *Escape*, Jill Stevens of *Kent Messenger* and Hilary Robinson of *Good Housekeeping*, for their comments and quotes; Christopher Priest of Ansible Information for getting my computer going just in time; Nick Wright of Editor Software and Richard Bailey of Lotus for their advice on the section about computing; writing tutor Dr Hilary Johnson of the London School of Journalism who helped me years ago to write in a language which was not my mother tongue; members of Konstanz Scriptease Writers Group, Wembley Writers, Darenth Writers, Tunbridge Wells Writers, Tonbridge

Scriptease Writers Group and Hastings Writers Group, all of whom helped me in some way or another with my freelance writing; Gareth Shannon of the Society of Authors who checked my contracts; Nick Phillips for his patient support; my friend and mentor and former chair of the Society of Women Writers and Journalists, the late Pamela Hutchings, who provided the inspiration for this book.

The case studies are based on fictitious characters. They have been chosen to represent typical situations, but any similarity of names is coincidence. The magazines used for sample letters exist only in the imagination of the author. Of course, the freelance journalists quoted in Chapter 13 are real people, and so are the editors who give their generous advice at the end of most chapters.

Christine Hall

1
Planning Your Success

Freelance journalism is one of the few hobbies which doesn't cost a lot of money. It can even be self-financing or profitable.

You can expand it into a freelance career: as a journalist you are independent, you can work from home, meet interesting people and earn a good income.

Many would-be writers dream of this career, but few succeed. They are talented, and may even have a few **articles** published, but they cannot achieve the big break-through. Perhaps you are among them.

As an editor, I have accepted hundreds of articles for newspapers, trade and consumer magazines, and rejected thousands. I know that many of these aspiring writers could break into print and make regular sales if they had an idea of what editors really want.

WHY WRITE ARTICLES?

There are almost 10,000 magazines and newspapers published in the UK alone, and most of them buy freelance manuscripts.

It is easier to break into print with articles than with short stories, and it is easier to make a living too. Most magazines publish only one story per issue, but dozens of articles, and most newspapers and trade magazines carry only articles. Editors can reprint a good short story after many years, but an article, however well written, becomes outdated, so the editor has to buy up-to-date material.

WHY DO EDITORS USE FREELANCES?

In a difficult economic climate, when publishers face losses in both advertising and subscription revenue, editorial budgets are cut back to a minimum. Less money is available to a constantly increasing number of aspiring contributors, including redundant staff journalists. Established

13

writers receive less **commissioned** work, and newcomers find it almost impossible to break into the market. A hopeless situation? Certainly not.

Clever freelances can secure a share of the reduced editorial budget if they are aware of what type of **features** editors are looking for in difficult times.

The first contributions to be axed are the beautifully written ones — those which editors used to accept because of their witty or elegant style. Most of them are based on facts and anecdotes obtained from reference books. Staff journalists can write them better and cheaper.

Your sales will be affected far less if you have expert knowledge of a topic. You don't need a university degree in your subject: your experience in bringing up a handicapped child, in organising camping holidays for teenagers, or in repairing furniture, makes you an expert.

For the editor, it is cheaper to buy a feature from a knowledgeable freelance than to assign a staff writer to spend days or weeks on research.

Do you have what it takes?

Your success depends on four factors:

1.   Natural writing talent

2.   Learning the craft and the necessary skills

3.   Hard work, dedication and self-discipline

4.   Business sense and marketing skills.

You need some of each, but not necessarily in equal parts. If you are born with extraordinary writing talents, you need less time to learn the skills. If you are only modestly talented, you need more dedication and must concentrate more on learning the craft. If you don't have the self-discipline to write a lot, you can make up for it by using your excellent marketing skills to sell every piece you write.

There is little you can do about your natural writing talent. The more you possess, the easier it is to succeed.

The craft of writing articles, journalistic skills, as well as the business and marketing side, are aspects you can learn from this book.

Hard work, dedication and self-discipline are what you have to put into it yourself. For many aspiring journalists, the difference between success and failure lies in six words: 'I did not have the time.'

GETTING STARTED

All you need to set yourself up as a journalist is a typewriter, a pile of A4 paper, envelopes, stamps, a notebook and a pen, and access to a telephone.

Reference books, word processors, answering machines, headed paper and so on are useful, but not essential. You can add them as you earn money from your journalism. (See Chapter 12: Going Freelance.)

LEARNING THE CRAFT

This book teaches you all you need to know about the craft to get started as a journalist. If you enjoy the additional stimulation of a course, there are several possibilities.

Evening classes

Classes at a college or adult education centre don't cost a lot (about £35 for a term), and you get comments on your work from both the tutor and other participants. Set tasks motivate you to write regularly, and meeting other writers can be stimulating.

However, course tutors are rarely successful writers themselves. They can point beginners in the right direction, but advanced writers may get little out of the lessons. Courses tend to emphasize the pleasure of creativity more than professionalism, and you may spend time learning about areas of writing in which you are not interested.

Residential courses

If you need to get away from your daily environment (for example, from looking after small children) to concentrate on writing, residential weekend or one-week courses are ideal. However, they are relatively expensive (around £270 for four days), because you pay for meals and accommodation as well as for the tuition.

Beginners are probably better off with a cheaper adult education centre course, or simply with working through this book. But it makes sense to invest in a specialist course, such as travel writing, once you've reached intermediate or advanced level.

Organisers of residential writing courses include Flair For Words, Taliesin Trust, Millers House Hotel, Midlands Arts, The Arvon Foundation, Fen Farm, Dilling House and Belstead House. For these and other useful addresses, see page 157.

Full-time courses

Colleges offer one-year, full-time courses in journalism which are designed for students who need a qualification to become staff journalists. These courses concentrate on the theory, but offer little practical help in getting your work published.

There are also shorter NCTJ (National Council for the Training of Journalists) courses, which are useful for journalists who have the experience but who need the theoretical knowledge about law or court reporting to pass the exam.

For people trying to get into the industry, PMA Training runs a nine-week course aimed at getting people jobs in either newspapers or magazines. 'Because we help people to get jobs after the course, and because we can pick and choose candidates, this course has a 100 per cent success rate,' explains Keith Elliott, PMA partner. This year there were over 1,000 applicants for the 24 places.

PMA also runs two- and three-day courses aimed at writers at basic, senior and advanced levels, for example: News Writing, Feature Writing, How to Interview, Sharpening Your Style, Law for Journalists. These courses are geared towards the practical needs of journalists. However, they are not cheap. A one-day course costs about £240 plus VAT.

Correspondence courses

You get your tuition by post and don't waste your writing time travelling to classes, and you can fit your studies into your daily routines. Correspondence courses are ideal for those who are bound to the house, for example handicapped people or parents of small children.

You have specified tasks to complete, and your tutor comments on your work and suggests improvements. The course material is usually very good, but success depends on your input. Learning by correspondence requires self-discipline and stamina; many students drop out.

Some organisers offer courses which cover the whole world of writing, including romantic novels and writing for children. You may prefer a shorter course which concentrates on journalism.

Michael Winckworth, Chair of The London School of Journalism, says: 'We have many students in the 18-30 age group who are professionals, working in some field in the media already, who want to get into journalism. They know exactly what they want, and usually complete the course.

'Then there are the type of students who have written a lot already, but are afraid of exposing their work to the criticism of a writers' group or evening class. They are often our most successful students, although they may decide not to complete the course.

'We also have people who move around a lot, for example in the army, for whom a correspondence course is the only way to get continuous tuition.'

Correspondence schools include: The London School of Journalism, The Writers Bureau, and The Writing School. Expect to pay around £200 for a one-year course.

Criticism services

Some writers offer to read and criticise your work for a fee. This service is useful if you cannot get honest criticism from another source, for example if you suspect that your spouse and your neighbours praise your work because they are too kind to tell you the truth.

The advice is only as good as the person who gives it. Check out the consultant's experience both in providing criticism and in getting published.

Remember that criticism obtained from these sources will be honest, but not necessarily frank. No consultant wants to lose a client. Instead of saying 'This piece is poorly written and boring', they write:'This feature shows great potential for improvement. . .'.

Consultants show you how to structure your article better, how to make the most of quotes or how to trim the piece down to saleable length, but they cannot sell your work for you.

Professional advice is not cheap. Expect to pay around £20 per article (less if you send in several at the same time).

For your first attempts at writing, listening to the comments from the members of your writers' group is cheaper. But once you've mastered the basics a professional's comments can be valuable.

Criticism services include: Jane Baker (The Writers Advice Centre), Hilary Johnson, Flair For Words, Christine Hall (Scriptease Editorial).

Writers' groups

Joining a writers' group is the cheapest way to get advice, honest and fair criticism, extra motivation and a boost to your social life. You can find out about writers' groups in the area from your local library or from the *Directory of Writers' Circles*. You can also start your own group.

Each writers' group works differently. Hastings Writers' Group, for example, meets every other week, either to discuss their own work, or for a talk given by a professional writer. Tunbridge Wells Writers'

Circle organises monthly talks by VIP authors, and runs sub-groups for journalism, short stories, novels and poems. Darenth Writers in Sevenoaks meet monthly to read aloud their latest work and invite comments.

Many other writers' groups, however, are little more than coffee and gossip circles. If the members are not committed to writing, and if you haven't learnt anything at the end of a meeting, you are better off at home, writing.

Postal workshops

If there is no writers' group in your area, you can join a postal group. Each time a parcel of manuscripts arrives, you take out your previous contribution, add your latest work, and write your opinion on the other people's work on a comment sheet. These postal workshops are great fun, and you get honest and fair criticism for little more than the cost of the postage stamps.

Depending on the size of the group and the efficiency of the members, it can take a while for the parcel to make a round. Contact addresses can be found in the *Directory of Postal Workshops.*

Writers' magazines

There are several excellent magazines for writers, and it is worth subscribing to at least one of them. Each time an issue arrives, crammed with ideas, advice, information on competitions and suggestions about where to sell your articles, your writing gets a big motivation boost.

Quartos, a bi-monthly magazine, offers probably the best value for money, with features about different forms of writing, interviews with publishers and authors and competition news. *Writers News* appears monthly and contains the most up-to-date information on writing competitions. *Writing Magazine* is aimed at beginners and is the only writing magazine you can buy at the newsagents. *Freelance Writing & Photography* and *Writers' Monthly* are also worth reading. *UK Press Gazette* is interesting for professional journalists only.

Members of a writers' group can share a subscription, or persuade the local library to stock these magazines.

OVERCOMING WRITER'S BLOCK

Writer's block is the name for the feeling that you cannot write anything, that you are empty, that you cannot come up with creative ideas or produce anything worth reading. Causes include tiredness, stress, great expectations or other pressures, lack of confidence or laziness.

Other languages have no phrase for this state of mind. Perhaps the writers in other countries don't suffer from this problem.

Strangely, the symptoms only affect freelance writers. Staff reporters never seem to have writer's block. They would not keep their jobs for long if they did.

Here are some tried and tested methods for overcoming writer's block.

- Set certain hours a day aside for writing every week. Lock the door, take the phone off the hook and sit down at your typewriter.

- Imagine that you are your own employer. Hire yourself for the day (or hour), and make sure that your employee gives his or her very best during this time.

- Imagine that you are a staff reporter and have to report to your editor or publisher at the end of the day.

- When you find it difficult to concentrate, go for a half-hour brisk walk, whatever the weather, to clear your mind. Then return to your typewriter.

- Whenever you go through a non-creative phase, use the time for all those essential non-writing activities: filing, writing query letters, sending invoices, research, market study.

- Set yourself a deadline. The average journalist is most productive writing under pressure.

DEVELOPING YOUR PERSONAL FIVE-YEAR PLAN

Where do you want to be in five years? What do you want to have achieved by then? Close your eyes and imagine the situation. Write down every detail.

Then decide how much you want to achieve in each of the five years leading up to that big target. Write down your targets, leaving a lot of space to jot down ideas of how you can achieve them. Write down all ideas as they come over the next few months. This book will provide many suggestions.

The most successful strategy for a beginner to become a professional freelance journalist has five phases: see Fig. 1 on page 20.

> **You are a professional and ready to go freelance**

PHASE 5
Learn marketing skills. Develop a business plan. Invest in basic office equipment. Increase your minimum rate to £50 per 1000 words. Try to break into markets which pay much more.

> **You know your markets and have built up contacts, and are selling your features regularly. You could say 'I'm a part-time writer'. Move on to phase 5.**

PHASE 4
You develop gradually from a hobby writer to a professional. Concentrate on your best paying markets, and write mostly for them. Put a price on your work. Write only for publications which pay at least £20.

> **Some editors recognize your name as a specialist writer and they value your contributions. Move on to phase 4.**

PHASE 3
Your aim is to get published in as many different magazines and newspapers as possible, with your byline.
Start specializing in one or several subjects. Join a writers' organisation and have headed paper printed.

> **When you've had at least ten articles published for payment, move on to phase 3.**

PHASE 2
Get as many articles published for payment as possible.
It does not matter how much you earn. If your payment is not more than £5 for an article in a small magazine, or a food hamper for the best readers' letter in a women's magazine, that's fine.

> **When your portfolio contains at least ten published articles, move on to phase 2.**

PHASE 1
You learn the craft, picking up advice from professional journalists and from books.
Your target is to get as many pieces published as possible.
It does not matter what they are, where they appear or if you get paid for them.
Building your portfolio must be your priority.

Fig. 1. Step by step from hobby writer to professional journalist.

How long does it take?

It all depends on you, on how much time and effort you are willing to spend. Five years is a realistic target if you have a full-time job, or are looking after a family with small children, but dedicate most of your spare time to writing.

If you can apply yourself to writing full time, you can make it in two years. On the other hand, if you regard writing as a hobby you can spend more time on phases one, two and three, and skip phases four and five altogether.

CASE STUDIES

Matt

The 'A' level student is determined to be a newspaper journalist. He knows that he won't find a junior reporter's job with a newspaper unless he has completed a course at journalism college, and that he won't get a place at college unless he has something to offer which other applicants don't have — such as a portfolio of published articles.

Matt is prepared to work hard and do a lot of writing in his spare time in order to have as many articles as possible published by next year, when he will apply for a college place. He will learn to touch-type to produce professional-looking **manuscripts**.

Cathy

This trained secretary and mother of three children wants to work from home. She needs the income, but also the flexible work hours which will allow her to look after her children, one of whom is disabled. She owns a word processor, and does some freelance secretarial work, but finds that mere typing doesn't satisfy her.

As far as she can remember, she has always been writing short stories, poems, letters and sketches. She has sent out some of her articles, but they all came back with rejection slips: 'The editor has read your article with interest, but regrets he cannot use it.'

Now Cathy wants to find out where she went wrong, and what editors really want. She considers signing up for a correspondence course. Her dream is to see her **byline** in a women's magazine.

Nigel

A trained mechanic who has worked both in production and as a service engineer for household appliances, Nigel was made redundant two years ago. At 48 it seems that most employers consider him too old, and many refuse to take on a long-term unemployed person anyway.

One of his previous jobs had included writing user manuals for household appliances, and he knows that he is good at explaining technical matters in plain English. He has heard that technical authors earn well.

Nigel is keen to prove that, whatever his age and however long he has been out of work, he can do worthwhile and profitable work. He is determined to get away from the dole. He gives himself one year to learn the craft, and hopes to earn a living in the second year.

Nigel doesn't have the money to pay for courses, so he joins a local writers' group to find out how other writers managed to break into print.

Joan

Recently retired, Joan enjoys gardening and needlecraft. Because of her natural curiosity she knows everything that's going on in the village — and what she doesn't know, she always finds out. Her friends call her a 'finder-outer'.

Joan likes the intellectual stimulation of interviewing people and writing, and has had a few articles published. She gets a big thrill out of seeing her work in print and would like it to happen more often, but she is easily distracted and never seems to have the time for writing. She has enrolled for an adult education centre course in Writing to Get Published, mostly because she wants to socialise with people who share her hobby, and to be 'pushed' to write more regularly.

WHAT THE EDITORS SAY

Several editors who are in the market for freelance material are offering their advice to the readers of this book:

- Jane Simon, commissioning editor of *Woman:* 'If you want to write for us, read the magazine every week to understand the type of **stories** that are suitable for *Woman.*'

- Charlotte Collis, editor of *Popular Crafts Magazine:* 'Write to magazines and newspapers and ask them for guidelines. There is no point wasting time on an article if it is not what the editor wants. Ask questions first — then write to brief.'

- John T Wilson, editor of *Great Ideas:* 'Find out what it is that particular editors want. Be reliable and open to their suggestions. Don't flood an editor with more stuff than s/he can use.'

- Martin Oxley, editor of the *Kent & Sussex Courier:* 'Learn to pester editors without annoying them.'

- Erika Harvey, editor of *Here's Health:* 'If you send unsolicited articles, don't expect a quick response. Don't hassle the editor, and don't think you can hand over a personal anecdote and sell it as hard-hitting journalistic reporting.'

- Suzanne Riley, editor of *Quartos:* 'Don't be afraid to experiment with different styles before you seriously decide whether you want to be a novelist, short story writer or journalist. Keep an open mind until you've learned the intricacies and techniques behind the craft of freelance writing.'

- Brian Attwood, editor of *The Stage and Television Today:* 'Take the trouble to analyse the paper. Don't waste office time asking for guidance when a proper read of a single issue will enlighten you. If your **copy** is substantially altered for length or style, then acquaint yourself with the changes you need to make.'

- Alan Travell, editor of *Freelance Writing & Photography* and *Escape:* 'Read a lot, write a lot, buy lots of stamps. Impress the editors with productivity. If they get regular submissions from you, they will start looking at your work with different eyes.'

2
Finding Out What Editors Want

Most freelances are surprised that editors are initially more interested in the idea for a feature than in the style in which it will be written. The explanation is simple: editors use freelances because they have fresh ideas, background knowledge, and access to information or contacts which the editors don't have.

Freelance features are valued for their content, not their style. An experienced subeditor can correct minor grammatical errors or a clumsy style within a few minutes. But no staff journalist can write the Marriage to a Belly Dancer feature as vividly and competently as the freelance whose brother is married to a professional performer.

KNOWING WHICH FEATURE IDEAS SELL — AND TO WHOM

You know that you can write. Your features are well structured, and thoroughly researched and topical. Your creative writing tutor encourages you to send them out. Yet all they bring in is a note saying 'The editor has read with interest . . . but regrets.'

What's wrong? There are three possible reasons:

1. You are sending your work to the wrong publications.

2. You are writing about the wrong subjects.

3. You are approaching your features from the wrong angle.

DOING MARKET RESEARCH STEP BY STEP

Ninety-five per cent of all articles are being rejected because they are not suitable for the newspaper or magazine to which they were sent. This means that in ninety-five out of one hundred cases the writers

24

could have saved themselves a lot of time and frustration by reading the publication before sending their manuscripts out.

Beginners develop an article idea first, then write the article, then send it to a magazine and hope for the best.

Professionals decide first about the magazine for which they want to write, then they analyse the publication and its readers, then they develop the idea and suggest it to the editor, and finally, they write the article.

Beginners send their work to the magazines they can see at their newsagents — with the result that a small number of national magazines are flooded with manuscripts.

Professionals write for specialist publications which are often known to insiders only, and which are constantly looking for competent writers.

Where to find your market

How many newspapers and magazines can you find on your local newsagent's shelves? One hundred? Two hundred? All of them are, of course, prospective markets. But the most likely markets are those which you don't see at the average newsagents.

Have a look at either the *Writers' Handbook* or *Writers' and Artists' Yearbook*. Each lists publications which use freelance material, complete with editor's name, address, and basic information about what material is being accepted; for example, 'Articles of relevance to small farmers about livestock and crops; items relating to the countryside considered'. Sometimes they even include the usual rate of pay.

Even better are *Benn's Media Directory* and *Willings Press Guide*. Both have separate volumes for the UK and for Europe, and list around twenty thousand publications. The information is targeted at people in the advertising industry, but journalists worth their salt can derive more from advertising information than from any other data. From the precise definition of the readership, for example 'All amateur and serious photographers', or 'Cosmetics, perfumery and toiletries buyers within multiple and independent chemists, relevant department stores and counter assistants', it is easy to decide if you can write for that publication, and if so, you can write your article with these readers in mind.

You don't have to buy these books when you set out to become a writer. Most public libraries have either the *Writers' and Artists' Yearbook* or the *Writers' Handbook*, and either *Benn's Media Directory* or *Willings Press Guide* in stock. However, once you're past the 'hobby writer' phase and serious about earning money from your writing, these books are an excellent investment.

Publication Analysis

for (name of publication):

Address:	Contacts (names and positions)
Frequency (eg, monthly:)	Rates paid (if known)
Average words per feature:	Average words per sentence:

How many of the articles in the sample issue could I have written? Which?

Is there an article to which I could add extra information, or a new angle?

How many articles are freelance written (that is, with byline of people not listed in the masthead)?

Which subject or subject group dominates the magazine (for example, fashion, health)?

Which subject group dominates the letters page of the current issue? (The editor will respond quickly to readers' requests and buy articles on those subjects)

Does the editor's comment column mention a change in editorial policy (always a great chance for new writers)?

Fig. 2. Publication analysis form.

Analysing your markets

Read at least one issue of a magazine to get the flavour before you develop an article idea for it. Then study at least two recent issues in depth before you submit your article, or approach the editor with an idea. Each time you consider writing for a publication, go through the checklists Publication Analysis (Fig. 2, page 26) and Readership Profile (Fig. 3, page 28). You can photocopy the checklists and fill them in.

Keeping the cost down

Market research can be expensive, especially if you have to buy several issues of many publications, and perhaps their main competitors as well, to study the difference in style and approach.

Particularly with glossy monthlies and trade magazines, costs add up quickly — and there is no guarantee that an eventual sale will cover the expenses.

However, there is no need to buy every magazine which might, or might not, be a market for you, from the newsagents. Here are some alternatives:

- Many charity shops sell second-hand magazines. They may not include the titles you were after originally, and they may not be the latest issues, but they are cheap. At 5p or 10p per copy you can probably afford to buy all the issues of a year or two and study the publication in depth.

- Ask all your friends and relatives not to bin any newspaper or magazine before you've seen it. You'll quickly build up a collection of titles of which you had not even heard. Some of them are better markets than the obvious titles on the newsagent's shelves.

- Your reference library has a stock of magazines and newspapers for you to read free. Most librarians are happy to dig out past copies for you. If the publication of your choice is not included, it's always worth asking for it. Librarians try to buy the publications which are demanded by their readers.

- Libraries regularly discard their old stock, usually after a year. Back copies are sold to regular buyers. You can obtain a subscription to your favourite magazine for 50p instead of £5 per issue. Editorial requirements don't change radically within a year.

Readership Profile

for (name of publication):

Male/female?	
Average age:	**Room for picture of typical reader (cut out from editorial or advertising pages)**
Marital status:	
Typical level of education:	
Any children? If yes: how many? Age group?	

Reader's (or family's) annual income:

Description of accommodation:

Hobbies:	Job/profession:

What are the reader's main problems?

If I was having tea with the typical reader, what would we talk about?

Which of my hobbies or professional interests are of interest to the reader?

If I was appointed editor of this publication, what would I do to make it essential reading for the typical reader?

Fig. 3. Readership profile form.

- Libraries discard their out-of-date reference books, too. The bigger the libraries are, the sooner they replace books. Ask your librarian. You can buy last year's issues of the two volumes of *Willings Press Guide* or the three volumes of *Benn's Media Directory* for around £10 — new, they would cost about £150.

- When sending out your query letter, ask the editor for 'back issues and damaged copies'. This works most of the time. Every editorial department has some shabby-looking back issues with missing pages lying around which sooner or later end up in the bin. Frequently, publishers miscalculate the exact amount of copies required for a particular issue, and the cupboards spill over with unwanted copies.

- To obtain a free up-to-date issue, write to the distribution department asking for a sample of the magazine. Publishers are always keen to oblige a prospective subscriber.

TEST: CAN YOU SENSE A GOOD STORY?

Try a little test: what would you make from this information?

Back in the days of the steam railway, the Redhill Railway brought prosperity to Little Redhampton. In 1952 it was no longer considered profitable and closed down, despite protests from Little Redhampton's citizens. In 1993 Rosalind Roundmouth, retired schoolteacher from Little Redhampton, bought what was left of the tracks and grounds. A newly founded organisation — The Redhill Railway Revival Club — raised funds to contribute towards the purchasing price. Under the guidance of a retired car mechanic, the Redhill Railway Revival Club rebuilt the line between Little Redhampton and Darkoak Green, and restored badly damaged engines. The railway opened in 1995 as a new tourist attraction. The interest from both locals and tourists has exceeded expectations by far. It appears that the new Redhill Railways is soon going to become a profitable enterprise. Its first anniversary is approaching.

Take ten minutes to jot down all feature ideas which come to your mind. Don't read on before you've done this exercise.

The possible ideas can be arranged in five main groups.

1. The history of the Redhill Railway. Little Redhampton in the time of the Redhill Railway. The history of the steam railway, etc.

2. Why it is important to revive Redhill Railway. Why we need more courageous citizens like Rosalind Roundmouth. Why Redhill Railway never should have closed down. Why we have to preserve our local heritage.

3. How the engines and carriages were restored. How to repair badly damaged historical engines. Technical difficulties in re-using old tracks. Case study of how one particular train is being restored.

4. The business side of the enterprise. Promotion strategies for the Redhill Railway venture. Finance and calculation of the venture. How to get a bank loan for a seemingly hopeless business venture. How to make money by re-opening historical monuments and railways.

5. A personality profile of initiator Rosalind Roundmouth. A personality profile of the car mechanic who was responsible for the restoration of the engines.

Tick the group (or groups) of subjects to which your ideas belong, then decide which of your feature ideas you would tackle first, before reading on.

Most freelance writers would go for number 1 and number 2. Most editors want number 5! Some editors, depending on the type of publication, will select number 3 or number 4.

This gap between supply and demand accounts for many rejections. Most editors receive piles of submission on 'The history of. . .' and opinion features, for which they have little use, but they rarely get enough material of the sort they really want.

If you switch to the following subjects, your number of acceptances will multiply immediately.

Personality profiles

Each time you read a news article or hear about an interesting event, ask yourself: who is the woman or man behind this? Why did they do it? How did they achieve it? What obstacles did they have to overcome? What effects does this event have on their lives? Interview them, and base your feature on this interview. Personalities need not be famous, but they have to be interesting. Don't structure a personality profile like a CV; concentrate on recent and current events. Remember that quotes characterise a person better than descriptions.

Features on royalty

True, the chances that Prince Charles agrees to an interview with you and reveals all about his love-life are small, but with a bit of thought you'll come up with feature ideas which can be linked with royalty. When I was editing a local paper, a freelance offered a feature about a local artist who had been commissioned to paint the Queen's racehorses. I accepted immediately. The writer was a beginner — but she certainly had journalistic instinct!

Anything to do with sex

There is no better way to increase a magazine's sales than sex in the headlines! Editors are well aware of it, but are concerned about the standards of their magazines. Pornography is the last thing they want.

Help them in their dilemma. Find a respectable subject related to sex, and give it a very sexy title.

In women's magazines, health, beauty, love, marriage, family planning, sports and children are legitimate frames for sex articles. It should not be difficult to come up with a number of ideas: Better Skin Through Better Sex, Sexually Transmitted Diseases. Or try How to Create a Really Sexy Bedroom. Travel articles often investigate the sex lives of women abroad. Many women's magazines publish interviews with strippers, male escorts or brothel managers.

A look at the cover of *Company Magazine,* which is aimed at 18-30-year-old women, shows the following headlines: Highway Hookers — Where 12-year-old Girls have Sex for £10, I've Slept with over 200 Men and Sexy Christmas Games for Grown Up Girls.

Marie Claire's cover boasts the following titles: Why Russian Women Consult Witches on Sex, My Brother is My Lover and We Have a Child, The Nun Who Became a Stripper, Twin Sisters, Now Brothers (about sex change), and Why We Need a School for Sex.

Sex is welcome in virtually every magazine or newspaper, provided it is handled with taste and targeted at the publication's particular readership and style. Photography magazines run lavishly illustrated features on nude photography.

The same recipe works for trade and business publications. When I was acting editor of *European Frozen Food Buyer*, I ran a feature on how erotic advertising campaigns boost the sales of ice cream. A reader survey showed that this was the most popular article in the magazine.

The list of possible feature subjects, ranging from The Effects of Consumer Advertising in Sex Magazines to How Male Employees are Sexually Harassed by Female Bosses is endless. It is up to you to come up with the right ideas — and don't forget, they must be respectable! Sex in the headlines helps sell a publication. Find a respectful way which suits the publication's style of including the subject in your feature.

Human interest stories

It is in our human nature to enjoy a bit of gossip, to find out how other people live and to form our opinion about them. True stories are much in demand by local newspapers and women's magazines. True stories must be true, and most magazines will insist on taking photos and using real names. Don't confuse them with first person 'confessions' which are often written by fiction writers.

Think of all the amazing things which have happened in your neighbourhood or family. The dog which returned after having been missing for five days. The baby which the doctors thought had died in the mother's body but was born and is perfectly healthy. The secretary who lost her job, received four hundred rejections to her application letters and, just when she was about to give up hope, was headhunted for a prestigious PA job in Paris. The aunt who bought a painting at a car boot sale for 60p and found out it was worth £3,000.

The ideal human interest story is about ordinary people with whom the readers identify, people who experience problems which could happen to the readers and who in the end, through luck or through their own determination, overcome a dreadful fate. This type of feature is called a 'tot' (triumph over tragedy).

WRITING WITH THE READER IN MIND

The average reader of *What Personal Computer* is male, 30-40 years old, interested in PCs which help him run his business, and he reads the publication to find out how to get them to work more efficiently. *PC Magazine*, on the other hand, is aimed at people who make computer purchase decisions in working/business environments.

The typical *Chat* reader is a 25-40-year-old, lower middle class housewife with one child and a part-time job. She spends much of her time reading magazines and watching television, and enjoys doing competitions. Another women's magazine, *Good Housekeeping*, targets women in their forties who belong to the middle and upper classes, who have a strong sense of home and family, and like cooking, entertaining and travelling.

Active Life is written mostly for the energetic, upper middle class female over 50. *Here's Health* readers are mostly middle and upper class females over 34, interested in alternative healthcare.

The *Kent and Sussex Courier* is read by the whole community, yet the editorial team writes with a typical reader in mind: a 35-year-old secretary from Tunbridge Wells.

The editor of *Steam Classic* knows that his magazine is most popular with 40-year-old men, who are married, have a family and who are enthusiastic about locomotives.

Practical Fishkeeping has an upper middle class male, aged 34, as its typical reader. Another hobby magazine, *Stamp Lover*, targets men aged 40 and upwards, who belong to a middle to upper social group and who are interested in all aspects of philately. *Popular Crafts Magazine*, on the other hand, is aimed mostly at women aged 25 and upwards, who belong to a middle income group, who are creative, and interested in home and crafts.

When you write an article for a particular newspaper or magazine, write a description of the average reader on a piece of paper. Then cut out a picture of someone who fits this description from an old magazine (probably the one for which you want to write). Pin them both up on the wall over your desk, or tape them to your computer screen. Look at your reader while you are writing for her.

Of course, magazines and newspapers are read by people in different age groups and from different backgrounds; but by slanting the publication at the average reader the editor makes it successful. Every editor knows who her average reader is: if you write for this reader, you win the editor's approval.

MAKING FREELANCE JOURNALISM RECESSION-PROOF

Many editors find they have to run a magazine on a drastically reduced budget and are at the same time being urged by the publisher to develop a better editorial concept to win back readers! What type of freelance feature do they need?

Newspapers and magazines — hobby magazines in particular — are among the first items the average consumer will give up if she is short of money. Only business and finance magazines are flourishing, probably because they advise readers on how to increase their income.

If only the editors of the average women's or leisure interest magazines could find a way to present their publication as a profitable investment!

This is your chance. The following five subject groups are extremely popular with editors and readers.

Articles on how to save money

Every editor welcomes original articles on this subject. Slant your article at the particular readership. How to Save Money on Heating Bills could be successful with a senior citizens' magazine, How to Organise a Children's Birthday Party on a Budget, for a parenting publication. Or try:

- Cooking: A Dinner Party for Under £3 Per Person

- Health: How to Pay Less for Dentists' Bills

- Travel: Value for Money Family Holidays

- Cars: How to Pay Less for That Second-Hand Car

- Finance: Cut Your Banking Charges

- Lifestyle: Do Your Own Furniture Repair

- Housekeeping: How Much Can Be Saved by Switching to Supermarkets' Own Brands?

- Fashion: Dress for Less.

Have a look at Shirley Conran's book *Down with Superwoman*. It is a source of ideas on how to save money in everyday life, many of which could inspire features.

Similar features can be written for hobby and trade magazines, *eg* Where to Find Good Second-Hand Photographic Equipment.

There is only one limit to your 'how to save money' features campaign: more than ever the editors have to take the interests of their advertisers into consideration. The editor of a bridal magazine, which exists almost exclusively on the advertising revenue from the fashion industry, is unlikely to publish a feature on Make Your Own Wedding Gown and Save Money. Try not to undermine the main advertisers' interests.

Articles on how to earn money

Do you know someone who has made a hobby into a profitable job on the side? Someone who earns money by creating dolls, repairing video cameras, painting silk ties, sewing individual lace underwear, taking wedding photos or whatever? Interview them for a human interest story. Women's magazines are looking for profiles of such people. Or turn the material into a how-to article: How to Make Money from Wedding Photography.

Consider your own — and your friends' — hobbies and the skills involved. How could these skills be utilised to earn an income?

Articles on work and careers

How to find/keep a job, how to get a pay increase, how to become self-employed: these subjects are more topical than ever! How to Get a Rise and How to Dress for an Interview come up again and again. But it isn't enough to rephrase information from a library book. You need a fresh, original angle and an optimistic approach. Spice your article up with quotes from personnel managers. What about How to Know if Your Job is in Danger, or a feature about senior citizens who've successfully started a small business?

Articles on how to get public money

How can individuals, groups of companies obtain public money? Which grants, scholarships, sponsorships, subsidies are available? For whichever readership you are writing (business women, college students, teenage girls, families or senior citizens), there is public money available. Find out for your readers how much is available for whom, where they can get further information, and what they can do to be one step ahead of other applicants! Sources of money (and of information on how to get it) are large companies, borough councils, the national government, the EC, the UN, etc. This sector has hardly been discovered by freelances yet. The trick here is to write up the bureaucratic information in a lively, popular style.

Articles on 'little luxuries'

Marketing people have always claimed that certain 'little luxury' sectors are booming in a recession. These include apparently unnecessary items such as take-away food, frozen desserts and wines from the supermarket. Surprising? Not at all. People are going out less, and enjoying themselves at home instead!

Base your feature on this idea: A Chinese Evening at Home (based on a take-away meal); or Dinner for Two in the Comfort of Your Home.

Another industry sector particularly successful in recessionary times is video hire. It is cheaper, and perhaps more fun, for a group of people to gather in somebody's home and watch a film together, than to go to the cinema. Smart freelances will use this trend to sell a feature, *eg* How to Organise a Video Evening for Your Friends, covering the selection of the right film(s), suggestions for food and drinks, atmosphere, who to invite and estimated costs.

WHAT THE EDITORS SAY

- Hilary Robinson, features editor of *Good Housekeeping*, says: 'I get about one hundred manuscripts per month, of which less than ten per cent are suitable. The most frequent mistake writers make is they don't study the magazine, and they make inappropriate suggestions for features. I need more human interest stories, especially of the "triumph over tragedy" kind, and first person stories.'

- Jane Simon, commissioning editor of *Woman*, asks for 'more real life stories about women'. She too says that less than 10 per cent of all submissions are suitable, and her complaint about prospective contributors is: 'They often submit ideas or features that aren't suitable for the magazine. It is clear that sometimes they haven't even bothered to read the magazine.'

- Human interest is in short supply at *Chat* too. Deputy editor Mary Bryce promises: 'Human interest stories are always welcome. We would like some humorous stories as well.'

- At *Practical Fishkeeping*, managing editor Steve Windsor comments: 'Over ninety per cent of manuscripts have to be rejected because the writers have not read the magazine and don't understand the style and content.' He adds that he would like more features about 'natural environments of fish'.

- Charlotte Collis, editor of *Popular Crafts Magazine*, says: 'Many freelances don't give enough information in their query. To make a decision I need to see what they are talking about. If they enclose a clear photograph and an outline, I can reach an effective decision.' She would like more suggestions for home interior features.

- At *PC Magazine*, editorial secretary Kathryn Joyce explains: 'We never publish unsolicited material. But we keep it, in case the commissioning editors are looking for someone to write about a particular subject. We file all material for future reference, and send a standard letter after seven to ten days.'

- *Steam Classic* editor Peter Merring says: 'We are always open to fresh ideas.'

- Brian Attwood, editor of *The Stage and Television Today*, is tired of those writers who fail to 'read the paper and overcome their prejudices'. He adds: 'I have lost count of the number of people who offer recycled press releases consisting of seasonal production notes and assume I will agree these are newsworthy. Likewise "feature" writers who expect me to accept grossly overwritten articles of 3,000 words and don't bother to acquaint themselves with our normal subject matter. And I hate it when writers take the view they can foist third-rate rubbish so long as the word "theatre" appears somewhere in the article.'

  However, he is in the market for opinion and think pieces. These should be: 'Tabloid in the best sense. The sort of article self-confessed journalists can turn around in no time but which the majority of those who prefer the title "writer" rarely master.'

- Erika Harvey, editor of *Here's Health*, rejects more than 90 per cent for the same reason: 'Too many contributors have no knowledge of the magazine content, philosophy and style.' Thirty to fifty manuscripts of feature suggestions arrive every month.

- Martin Oxley, editor of *The Kent & Sussex Courier*, describes the typical error of a prospective contributor: 'Believing that a local paper would be interested in a travel article on Papua New Guinea.'

- 'Not knowing the style of the magazine' is the most frequent reason why hopeful contributors to *What Personal Computer* have their manuscripts returned, according to editor Gail Robinson.

- At *Active Life*, managing editor Helene Hodge explains: 'The main reason why I reject more than ninety per cent of freelance submission outright is that the writers clearly don't understand the market.' She adds that she is interested in getting more finance-related articles.

- Financial matters and investment advice are also in demand by *Great Ideas*. Editor John T Wilson gets between six and ten manuscripts per month, and he is in a luckier position than other editors as far as freelance submissions are concerned: 'More than half of the manuscripts which land on my desk are at least worth considering.' But he too gets his share of unsuitable material: 'Many writers don't bother to find out what our newsletter is like and what our needs are.'

- Suzanne Riley of *Quartos*, a magazine for writers, says: 'We can receive up to 300 manuscripts and proposals per month, more if you include mass poetry submissions. Of these only a handful get a second reading.

  'We are constantly looking for the snappy, original article that is going to inform and/or entertain the readers. The tired old chestnuts on Why I Write, or Papering the Wall with Rejection Slips, instantly get the blue pencil since they usually reflect an amateur or negative attitude to serious freelance writing.

  'We would like topical pieces on subjects like the net book agreement, the book price wars, authors' profits versus supermarket outlets, etc, but very few writers bother to offer us features of this type.

  'Having said that, the Booker Prize is done to death regularly every year — without the freelance ever going anywhere near a Booker nominee!'

- Alan Travell, editor of *Freelance Writing & Photography* and *Escape:* 'I get lots of articles which people wrote because someone told them to, perhaps as an exercise for a writing course. They are almost identical. The subject is good but the angle is boring. For example, "The ABC of . . .". Writing tutors still think editors want that sort of thing. But such an article would have to be really good.

  'For *Escape*, we have recently started including lifestyle features, but few contributors seem to realise that. I'm definitely looking for lifestyle material.

  'For *Freelance Writing & Photography*, articles can be targeted at beginners or at old hands, but they must not talk down to the reader.'

3
Writing the Irresistible Query Letter

Imagine you are being bombarded with unwanted mailshots. Day after day you find leaflets on double glazing, life insurance, garden furniture and antiques auctions in your post. Do you read them all? Most of them will go straight into the bin.

A week later, the garden furniture salesman phones and demands an explanation for why you have not decided yet whether to buy the set of garden chairs. You have never had a garden. Annoying, isn't it? What a waste of your time and patience.

You wish you could stop the flood of unwanted offers somehow, perhaps with a sign at your door saying 'Strictly no unsolicited material'.

This is exactly how editors feel when they receive a dozen or more unsolicited manuscripts every day. They have not asked for them, and they simply don't want them.

QUERY FIRST

Editorial staff look at every manuscript they receive, but they don't have time to read them from beginning to end. After all, they have a magazine or newspaper to produce. Reading freelance manuscripts is a very minor part of an editor's job. It is usually left until there is time for it (and there never is). In the end it is often a secretary or trainee who sorts out the slush pile and returns at least the obvious rejections.

The editor has a quick look to see if the subject and angle of any of the remaining manuscripts are interesting and useful to her publications. In most cases, they are as useful as the brochure on garden furniture in your post if you don't have a garden. The freelances have wasted their time.

Every editor likes to be approached in a different way. Most feature editors prefer a query letter with synopsis, which is so much quicker to read than a whole manuscript.

Nigel Nickeling, Journalist

1, Abcde Lane
Fghijkl Town YY1 1ZZ
Tel (0000) 0000

Doreen Dorian,
Editor 'You and Your House'

15 July 199x

Dear Doreen Dorian,

I am a regular reader of You and Your House. As a qualified mechanic and experienced DIY
enthusiast, I have come up with some ideas for your magazine. I used to write technical instructions for a household appliances firm and can explain technical matters in plain English. Would
you be interested in the following:

1. How to prevent costly plumbing disasters. Step by step instructions on how to prepare your
plumbing system for the winter. What to do if disaster strikes (frozen pipes etc), with a 'what if'
checklist. Targeted at the reader who knows little or nothing about the subject.

2. How to make your home burglar-proof. Ten clever ways to keep burglars out, costing little or
nothing. Did you know, for example, that fifty per cent of all burglars break in through the
ground floor back windows? It can cost as little as £5 to fit these windows with locks. With brief
comments by a senior crime prevention officer and 'did you know' facts in a box.

3. How to save money on heating bills. You can reduce your household heating costs by up to
50%. Twenty ideas how to keep those costs down this winter, each with clear 'how-to'-instruc-
tions and approximate costs.

SAE enclosed. I look forward to hearing from you.

Yours sincerely

Nigel Nickeling

Nigel Nickeling

Fig. 4. Query letter (1).

Please don't phone: your phone call is bound to come at a moment when everyone in the editorial department is desperately trying to get the final pages ready for print! Of course, there are always exceptions to the rule. If you know that a particular editor prefers phone calls, or if the subject is topical, then ring them, but don't waste their time. Be clear in your mind about the feature you want to write, and how you would develop it, before you phone.

PLANNING THE CONTENTS OF THE QUERY

The type of query letter to which most editors respond favourably contains the following information:

1. The subject, as precisely as possible. Many freelances make the mistake of suggesting a subject in too general terms. For example, don't offer a feature on Belly Dancing, but on How to Become a Professional Belly Dancer, or How Belly Dance Can Help Slimming, or The World's Oldest Belly Dancers.

2. The angle. For example, personality profile of Nefertiti Osiris who is a professional performer, or advice for enthusiastic amateurs.

3. The style. For example, humorous, informative, light-hearted, factual, scientific.

4. The contacts who will be quoted. Their names, positions and, if appropriate, their relationship to you, such as 'Sheharazad Humperdinck, my sister-in-law, who has been a professional performer for eleven years'.

5. The suggested length, *eg*: 900-1000 words.

6. The author's qualifications to write on the subject, for instance: 'I am a member of the Midlands Arabic Dance Network and have been teaching belly dancing for five years.'

7. The expected payment. Remember you are offering a service — like the double-glazing sales person who dropped the leaflet into the letterbox. State your price. The editor won't take this for greed.

Cathy Clever, Freelance Journalist
'Scribbles', 11 Abc Drive, Xyzzyx 1YW WYA,
Tel & Fax: (0000) 0000
Member of the Society of Women Writers and Journalists

Sabrina Sunday, Features Editor
Suzanne Magazine

15 July 199x

Dear Ms Sunday,

Are you interested in a feature on what it is like to be the husband of a belly dancer? How does a man feel when his wife dances in a night-club, or gives 'bellygram' shows at private parties? Does he mind when she gets fan mail from men who describe her dance as 'the most erotic, most exotic, most exciting' performance they have ever seen?

My brother, Stan Humperdinck, is in this situation. His wife, Sarah, dances professionally under the stage name Sheharazad. Stan acts as Sarah's agent, manager and accountant, and accompanies her to every show. He enjoys her success. It rarely happens, but there are occasions when he steps in if an eager admirer wants to do more than just watch!

I am familiar with the subject of belly dancing: I have been teaching oriental dancing at the local adult education centre for ten years.

I propose a 700 word feature with strong human interest and lots of quotes, and a 200 word fact file on belly dancing (as a boxed item), with payment at your usual rates. Sarah and Stan are willing to be photographed.

I enclose a stamped addressed envelope and I look forward to hearing from you.

Yours sincerely,

Cathy Clever

Fig. 5. Query letter (2).

On the contrary, it shows that they are dealing with a professional! If unsure how much to ask, write 'At your usual rates', or give a wide range such as 'My usual rates are between £30 and £110 per 1000 words.'

If the editor doesn't like the subject offered in the query letter, the freelance has not wasted much time. If the editor likes it, he or she can ask for alterations, such as a different angle or length.

The best query letters, however, are the ones which contain two, three, five, ten, twenty feature suggestions!

SAVING TIME

Suggestion lists are great time savers for the editor. They also show that the freelance has studied the publication, is interested in the subject and could become a regular contributor. All editors prefer regular contributors to one-off submissions, because it reduces the administrative work involved.

The editor can select the most suitable ideas and write a quick letter: 'Please send nos 3, 8, 13 and 16 on spec.'

DEAR EDITOR

How do you address an editor whose name you don't know? 'Dear Sir' is old-fashioned and will not endear you to a female editor. 'Dear Sir or Madam', 'Dear Madams and Sirs' and 'Dear Editor' are all acceptable.

It is, though, always worth finding out the editor's name, either by looking it up in the publication, or with a quick phone call. 'Dear Mr Smith' is correct, and 'Dear John Smith' is being used more and more frequently. 'Dear John', of course, is not acceptable until the editor has started signing his letters to you with 'Yours, John'.

When you get a reply from another member of the editorial staff, for example the features editor or the editorial assistant, it is a good idea to address your future letters to them directly.

Enclosing samples and SAEs

Query letters, as well as unsolicited manuscripts, must be accompanied by a stamped addressed envelope (sae). If you are sending something the magazine staff haven't asked for, you cannot expect them to pay for

Suzanne

Magazine

18 August 199x

Dear Ms Clever,

Thanks for your letter of 15 July. I am pleased to commission you to write the proposed feature about the belly dancer and her husband.

However, the overall length must not exceed 700 words, which must include a short boxed item. Please keep your sentences short and punchy. Can you include a mention how she got involved with belly dancing?

We need a selection of photographs (slides), showing Sheharazad during a show (if possible with fans), and at home with her husband. We will probably use two slides, but our picture editor would appreciate if you could submit at least ten.

The feature will probably be published in next year's March issue. Please send the manuscript no later than 30 September 199x. Our rates are £200 per 1000 words, plus £30 per published photo.

Please phone me or the editorial assistant, Julie Jiller, if you have any questions.

Yours sincerely

Sabrina Sunday
Sabrina Sunday
Features Editor

Suzanne Magazine Publishing. Ksf jdkjfdfj Akf, Bxxjdfjs Cdf jdfjksdjfds, 11 Ddfjskdf Efgh, Gfd sdkjf. EC1 1CE, Asdfdjsf Bdjfksdf Cdkf , Djfjsdkf Edkf Fds Gdsjfkd 0101010101, Hfdsjf ldfjs Jkdfs Lkfsdskdjf Telephone (00000) 000000, Telefax (00000) 0000

Fig. 6. Commissioning letter.

the return postage. However, if an article has been commissioned, or if the editor expressed an interest in your work and has asked to see it 'on spec', you don't need to enclose an sae.

It is fine to send a stamped, addressed 're-use envelopes' label instead of an envelope if you want to help the environment and keep costs down. Much-used, much-licked envelopes are not acceptable.

Don't send samples of previously published work at this stage. They only increase the height of the pile and the editor's unwillingness to look at it. Again, there are exceptions, and if you know that an editor likes to see published work, photocopy a couple of articles which are similar in style or content to the one you want to write.

GETTING COMMISSIONED

An editor who likes a feature idea will either commission you, or ask you to submit it on speculation (**on spec**). If you receive a go-ahead from an editor, make sure you know whether it is a commission.

If you are commissioned to write an article, it means that the editor promises to buy it and to pay for it. Editors tend to commission only writers who are well known, or who have contributed previously to the publication.

You need a letter confirming the agreement, including subject, deadline and price. If the editor commissions you over the phone, you can send a confirmation letter. See example on page 46.

Of course, once you are established as a journalist you will try to get as much commissioned work as possible, and only occasionally send your work out on spec.

SUBMITTING ON SPEC

In most cases the editor asks you to submit a feature on spec. Treat this as a sales opportunity, but don't regard it as an agreed sale. There is no guarantee that the editor will buy an article she has asked to see, but your chances are increased by about 500 per cent! You know that the editor is interested. Now your success depends on how well you write the article, and if you deliver the promise contained in your query.

As you become more experienced as a journalist, and the editors get to know your work, you should try to get more commissioned work instead of submitting on spec.

Nigel Nickeling, Journalist

1, Abcde Lane
Fghijkl Town YY1 1ZZ
Tel (0000) 0000

Doreen Dorian,
Editor 'You and Your House'

15 August 199x

Dear Doreen Dorian,

Thank you for your phone call, commissioning me to write the article 'How to make your home burglarproof'.

I am happy to confirm that you will have the article by 10 September latest, complete with the requested colour photo for illustration. You agreed to pay £50 for the 800 word article and £20 for the photo.

Yours sincerely

Nigel Nickeling

Fig. 7. Confirmation letter.

WILL THEY STEAL MY IDEA?

Fears that the editor could steal a good idea suggested in a query letter are common among beginners, but totally unfounded. It may happen that an editor rejects a feature because she has accepted a manuscript on a similar subject a week before, and then the freelance is under the impression that her idea has been copied.

But editors never steal ideas. Why should they? The freelance who has come up with the suggestion is always the best person to write the feature, because she is involved and motivated.

WHAT THE EDITORS SAY

● Gail Robinson, editor of *What Personal Computer:* 'I prefer a written synopsis.'

● Steve Windsor, managing editor of *Practical Fishkeeping:* 'A written synopsis, a phone call, or a complete manuscript — any of these is acceptable.'

● Jane Simon, commissioning editor of *Woman:* 'I like to see a written synopsis first. But if the story is currently in the news, it's best to phone me.'

● Helene Hodge, managing editor of *Active Life:* 'A written synopsis, please.'

● John T Wilson, editor of *Great Ideas:* 'Written synopsis.'

● Erika Harvey, editor of *Here's Health:* 'A written synopsis of the proposed article, plus a CV and articles published.'

● Martin Oxley, editor of *The Kent & Sussex Courier:* 'A complete manuscript.'

● Mary Bryce, deputy editor of *Chat:* 'Phone to discuss the idea before submitting a manuscript. The weeklies market is frantically busy, and it's very time consuming reading through manuscripts which are unsuitable.'

Starsheet

Dear Writer,

We have read, with interest, your article/short story/letter/idea. We regret that we are not able to use it. We wish you best of luck in placing your work elsewhere.

Yours sincerely

The Editor

Starsheet Publications. Ksf jdkjfdflj Akf, Bxxjdfljs Cdf jdfjfksdjfds, 11 Ddfjskdf Efgh, Gfd sdkjf EC1 1CE, Asdfdjsf Bdjfjksdf Cdkf, Dfjfsdkf Edkf Fds Gdsjfkd 0101010101, Hfdsjf lufljs Jkdfs Kkdjfs Lkfsdskdjf,Telephone (00000) 000000, Telefax (00000) 000000

Fig. 8. Rejection slip.

TRAVEL TIPS
The independent newsletter for family holidays

17 September 199x

Dear Cathy,

I have enjoyed reading your article, 'Ten Tips for Travelling with a Handicapped Child'. I plan to include it in the December issue, and pay our usual rate of £20 per 1000 words, on publication.

I would be interested in a series of articles, 'Ten Tips for...' each covering a different aspect of travelling. For example, travelling with a baby, travelling with a pet, etc., one per issue. The articles must be informative, and they can be humorous. If you are interested, could you please send some suggestions?

Yours sincerely

Toby

Toby Tinkerton
Editor

Newsletter Publishing, 11 Aksjfsdj Bakdjfkds, D dkfkdsf Rkjfium, Ekjdfu Acureure, Yuidfnsd,f, Udtnb 000000000, Wsdjfmvdrewec Tskdjr, Tel. (00000) 00000,Fax (00000) 000000

Fig. 9. Letter of acceptance.

- Hilary Robinson, deputy editor of *Good Housekeeping:* 'We prefer a phone call.'

- Ian Boughton, group editor of *Stationery Trade News* and other trade publications, invites suggestions for fresh feature ideas: 'I wish freelances would use their own imagination. It's astonishing how often I get asked exactly what I want written. If I knew that, I would write it myself.

  'On the other hand, if the editor commissions a feature it is a creative tactic to ask: "Do you have an angle on this, or is my brief a broad subject, and is it up to me to find a good angle for you?" This will earn a few points.'

4
Breaking into Print — Step by Step

BUILDING YOUR PORTFOLIO

At the beginning of your career it is important that you get articles published. It does not matter what and where at this stage, or if you get paid. Once you have had articles published, you can mention in your query letters 'I've had articles on this subject published in the local press', or 'I'm a regular contributor to *Belly Dancer*', which shows that you are not a beginner. It also enables you to send samples of published work should an editor want to see them.

Your clippings book

Buy yourself a clippings book as soon as you've had the first snippet published, and use it. Don't leave your published articles lying around — you are going to lose them!

Spiral-bound clippings books are more useful than those which are glued or stapled and can't be closed properly when a lot of clippings have been inserted. Ringbinders with A4 plastic pockets are practical, because you can rearrange the order of the sheets or take them out for photocopying. Choose something in A4 size or larger. The decorative books used for personal diaries are too small when it comes to magazine articles.

A portfolio of your published work is wonderfully motivating. Browsing through your own successes will cheer you up when you're feeling low after a period of rejection slips. And it will impress your friends and visitors, too.

WRITING READERS' LETTERS

A readers' letter is quick and easy to write, and easier to get published, if you know to do it. Aim at publications which have a low circulation. A special interest or club newsletter with 300 readers, or a free local

51

newspaper with a circulation of 70,000, receive far fewer readers' letters than a magazine like *Woman* with a circulation of around 700,000.

If you belong to a club or society which has its own newsletter, you know what interests or moves other members. Put forward a new idea, make suggestions for improvements, contradict what the writer of an article in the last issue has said.

Local newspapers are a great market for readers' letters. Send them a letter every week until they publish one!

Look around you, listen to what people are talking about at the post office, at the hairdressers, at parents' evenings at the school. Which are the local issues that you, or they, feel strongly about? Can you offer a new perspective, a new angle? Positive suggestions about how to deal with problems are always welcome. Don't be afraid to be controversial, or to present a view opposed to what everyone else seems to think. Local newspaper editors are happy to provide reading material which makes their readers think and talk.

A readers' letter is not a school essay, where you first state everything which supports one view, then everything which supports the other and weigh them up in the last paragraph for a well-balanced summary. State your view and stick to it.

Keep your letter short. Two or three hundred words are enough for a local paper. Put your main statement in the first paragraph, then add the arguments and reasons, with the most important ones first. Subeditors at local papers like to use readers' letters as fillers, and if a letter can't be squeezed into the available space they'll chop off the end.

The readers' letters which have the best chance of getting published are those which have a strong local flavour and a touch of humour. In summer, local papers receive fewer letters than in winter.

Readers' letters aren't usually paid for — although the best published letter in some magazines wins a food hamper or a pen — but they are a great way of building up a portfolio of published work.

Take your success with readers' letters seriously. It proves that you have a journalistic mind, that you can understand what interests the readers and what editors want, and that you are able to write and structure a piece well enough for a publication to print it.

WRITING FOR CLUB NEWSLETTERS, SCHOOL AND COLLEGE MAGAZINES

Are you ready to try your hand at articles and features? Think small, and write about what you know. Do you belong to a club, society or organisation which has its own newsletter or magazine? Such publications are often put together by volunteers who are glad of extra input.

Avoid moody 'think-pieces'. Put yourself in the position of the reader. What do you want to find in your newsletter? Subject related news and information! Write short articles which give the reader interesting information about what's going on, how to achieve better results with their hobby and so on.

Club newsletters usually don't offer payment, but they are generous with bylines.

CONTRIBUTING TO YOUR LOCAL PAPER

Local newspapers have to be run on smaller and smaller budgets. One reporter has to investigate and write about the same area which, ten or 20 years ago, was covered by five reporters.

If an aspiring journalist offers to supply local news stories free of charge, the editor will probably jump at the chance. However, this applies only to contributors who know what articles are needed and can write them well.

Hopeful writers who supply piles of poems about primroses in spring, extracts from their unpublished memoirs and praises of the uncle's shop are a nuisance. Every local newspaper editor is hassled by these ineffective time-wasters, and will assume that you belong to that category until you prove the opposite.

Short news articles of about 200-300 words, with a strong local flavour, human interest and an upbeat mood are most in demand. If a teenager in the neighbourhood has won a scholarship for Cambridge University, or departs with Operation Raleigh for adventures in the Amazon jungle, or if your neighbour is a runner-up in a national businesswoman-of-the-year award, it's worth writing about.

Write it up quickly, putting the basic facts in the first paragraph, add a couple of quotes and further information, and hand it in at the newspaper office. Enclose a note saying that the editor can use the article if the editorial space is available, and that you don't expect to be paid.

If you can enclose a photo for illustration, so much the better. But if getting photos developed means delaying submission of the article until it is no longer 'news', it's better to hand it in without a picture.

Don't be disappointed if not all your articles are being used. Sometimes newspapers have more news articles than editorial space, and give preference to staff-written ones. In other weeks the subeditors are hard pressed to find enough copy to fill the column, and they will gladly use your material.

Taking your chance in the 'silly season'

Have you noticed that, in certain months, photos are often blown up to a size which is in no proportion to their importance? This is because nothing newsworthy has happened and the subeditors don't have enough articles to fill the space. Every publication has its own 'silly season', when the silliest story is taken up and developed into a big article just to fill the space. For local newspapers this tends to happen in January, July and August.

This is your chance. Keep your eyes and ears open, and write an article about what is happening!

In the 'silly season' there is also a chance of getting a real feature in the local paper. This is usually based on an interview with a local person who does something unusual or interesting. (See Chapter 6: Structuring and Writing the Feature.)

How to become a village or club correspondent

Most local newspapers have special pages for 'village news' and 'club news'. This is because the readers are interested in who is the new chair of the Women's Institute or where the Horticultural Society is going for its next outing — but only if they are members of the group, or if the news refers to their own village. This type of news is therefore listed under the name of the relevant club or village.

Club correspondents are usually the press officers of the local clubs. Why not join a couple of clubs? They will probably be only too pleased to have you as a press officer, especially if you have already had a few pieces published.

Some newspapers cannot afford a reporter in every village, but don't want to miss out on the local news. Either they encourage their readers to send in news — which is an unreliable method — or they find a correspondent in each village. Let your newspaper editor know that you are an available correspondent if he ever needs one in your village!

The ideal village correspondent lives in the village, is well known by the residents, is lively and popular, and involved in local groups and events. He must have a telephone, so that neighbours can ring with news and the editor can ring with queries.

A village correspondent is expected to write three to five news items of one or two hundred words for each issue, and is paid about £8 per issue. Not a lot — but this is your first step towards real, paid-for journalism!

What do you write about? Subjects are not hard to find. Mrs Smith has won the tenth prize in a poetry competition; the Scouts are looking for a new leader; the horticultural society changes the venue for its monthly meetings; the camera club invites new members.

Subeditors often despair at the offerings of village correspondents. Their articles are too wordy, and they write lengthy intros before getting to the point. Flowery phrases and words such as 'lovely', 'delightful', are loved by the correspondents, but not by the subeditors who have to cut them out.

Keep your sentences simple and active. Write only about what interests your readers. They like to hear who talked about what, but not necessarily that the chairperson in a pea-green dress delivered a vote of thanks to the speaker who wore a purple hat.

Ten reasons to become a village correspondent

1. You can fill your **clippings book**.

2. Your **social life** becomes more interesting; you are a welcome guest at many events.

3. Your neighbours will approach you with **information** which you can use for articles for other papers.

4. You learn **interviewing skills**.

5. You acquire basic telephone liaison and research **skills**.

6. You learn how to present copy and how to follow a **house style**.

7. You get used to working to a tight **deadline** and to produce work under time pressure.

8. You are a 'real' journalist and **get paid** for your work.

9. The editor of your local newspaper gets to know **your name**.

10. Sometimes you are given free in-house journalistic **training**. Whenever the newspaper runs training sessions on writing style, libel or photography, ask if you can attend.

CASE STUDIES

Matt

After submitting a few short articles on amateur sports, of which the local newspaper published several, Matt offered to do some sports reporting. The sports editor of the local newspaper was delighted. 'Hurrah — here is someone who volunteers to attend sports events at weekends!'

For Matt, who spends much of his spare time watching football matches anyway, this occupation is more fun than work. The sports editor has no budget to pay Matt, but he gives him some useful tips on how to write about sports events without using clichés. On average, Matt writes one or two sports articles per week and his portfolio builds up quickly.

Cathy

When the local newspaper advertised for a new village correspondent — the previous one had moved — Cathy rang and offered her services. To her surprise, she was taken on immediately. She was the sort of person the editor wanted: a local who knew everyone. Through her children she is well connected with the local schools, and her occasional secretarial work has put her in touch with small local businesses. Every week Cathy's column is published, together with the byline and photograph, and once a month she gets a cheque. She has become a local celebrity who is welcome at every meeting.

She also approached the entertainments editor and offered to review theatre performances for children. 'This is great. I can take the children with me and need not find a babysitter. They love it, and their comments help me write the review. And, of course, we get free press tickets. I could not afford to take them to the theatre otherwise. We look forward to the Christmas panto season!'

One of the schools has asked her if she would like to contribute to a school newsletter, perhaps even edit it: another opportunity to fill her clippings book.

Nigel

Angry about delayed roadworks, Nigel wrote a letter to the local paper, which was published the following week. Encouraged by this success, he posted a letter every week. Several were published. One day the deputy editor rang him: 'We really like your letters, but we can't print them all. We must give space to other people as well.'

Nigel had the presence of mind to reply: 'I appreciate that. Would you like some news articles instead?' But when the deputy editor said: 'Why, what do you have in mind?' he was lost for ideas. However, he is now brainstorming for article ideas to suggest.

Joan

A member of the local Women's Institute and Horticultural Society, Joan offered these groups her services as a press officer. To her delight the local paper has published each of her press releases in the clubs and groups section. Many of them were drastically shortened, however. 'I realised that they did not want 800 words about a meeting, and wrote shorter, more concise articles.'

Joan is now considering joining the local ramblers' group. She has heard their chairperson mention that they need more publicity.

JOINING THE EDITORIAL TEAM

Most professional freelance journalists have one big advantage: they have inside knowledge of the publishing world. It is amazing how many of them, however briefly, have worked in a publishing environment, as staff journalists, reporters, subeditors, secretaries at a literary agency, editorial assistants, desktop publishing operators, proofreaders and so on.

This experience gives them an understanding of how magazines and newspapers are put together, how editors think and how manuscripts should be presented.

If you can spare a week or more, why not join your local newspaper for editorial work experience? Especially in summer, when many of the staff journalists are away on holiday, the editor may welcome help.

You could argue that unpaid work is labour exploitation, but from hands-on experience in an editorial office you will probably learn more than from a journalism course, for which you would have to pay a lot of money. And you are not taking away anybody's job, are you?

Practical experience in an editorial office gives you the edge over other freelances. You learn how an editor's mind works and a newspaper or magazine is put together. In addition, you can add a lot of articles to your portfolio of published work. You can also mention in query letters to other publications that you have experience in working for so-and-so newspapers — you don't have to mention that it was only for a couple of weeks!

Of course you have to convince the editor that, if he decides to take you on, you will be an asset to the office and not a bother. Editorial offices are frantically busy and staff will not have much time to look after you.

You can also apply for work experience placements with national newspapers or magazines, but these are more difficult to obtain.

CASE STUDIES

Matt

'It was easy to get a placement with the local newspaper because they had published my articles before. However, nobody had the time to explain a lot. I took the initiative and phoned up local charities, asking if they had any news, and turned the information into little articles. Most of these were published in the next issue.

'During my three weeks I answered the phone for the editorial team and did telephone interviews. I was also allowed to shadow one of the senior reporters. We went to the same events together, wrote separate articles and compared the results. He said I did well for a beginner, but I think I still have a lot to learn.'

Cathy

'I couldn't possibly leave my children on their own for a whole week, but my husband agreed to take a day off work and look after them. I wrote to one of the big national women's magazines and asked if I could spend a day in the editorial office. To my surprise, they agreed immediately.

'In the morning I helped the editorial assistants with the filing. We cut out articles from other magazines and sorted them by subject, so that whenever the editor decided to do a feature on a particular subject they had some information at hand.

'In the afternoon I worked for the commissioning editor. I sent out rejection slips to would-be contributors. What a feeling! I was astonished to see how many unsolicited manuscripts they had, and most of it was clearly unsuitable for a women's magazine. One writer had sent a whole collection of children's stories, although the magazine has never published anything for children!

'I also sent out cheques to regular contributors and updated their files. This was a real eye-opener. Some of them get £600 for a single article! I wouldn't mind earning that much.'

Nigel

'I found a one-week's placement with a drinks trade magazine. They gave me a huge pile of recent press releases, all about new products, and asked me to phone the producers to obtain additional information. I had to find out the launch date, the retail price, the quantity, the regional availability and the target consumer. I also had to ask for a photo and get a suitable quote from a senior person.

'I was talking to some pretty high-up people, and in many cases the producers were based in another country. Then I wrote them all up for the new products section of the magazine.

'One of my interviewees invited me to a press reception to introduce a new brand of sparkling wine. He had no idea I was only a work experience person! The editor laughed, and said I should go, as long as I came back with an interesting interview and did not expect to get paid for it.

'I went, just for the fun of it. We journalists were treated like royalty, wined and dined at a first class restaurant. Of course I didn't let on that I was a beginner! I listened in to one of the drinks journalists interviewing the marketing director about the label and design, and I asked some questions about their marketing strategies.

'At the end of the party I had more than enough material for an article. They even gave every journalist a press pack with photos and information about the company, as well as two bottles of the wine to sample at home.'

Joan

'I wrote to several magazines and got no reply. Then suddenly the fashion editor of a women's magazine phoned: they were doing a photo shoot the next day and would I like to stand in for her assistant who had been taken ill?

'They were taking photos of bridal gowns in the park-like grounds of a luxurious hotel. I found myself ironing hooped petticoats, making coffee, and selecting the accessories to go with the gowns. I took detailed notes of which dresses, accessories and cosmetics were used for which photo. We spent about two hours on each photo, and the whole shoot took two days.

'The next week the fashion editor invited me to the editorial office to help select the best pictures. There were hundreds of almost identical slides of each shot. We checked for unwanted shadows, for creases in the fabric of the gowns, for facial expression.

'Best of all, I was allowed to write the captions for this photo shoot! I was so excited when the magazine came out in print. The pages are now in my portfolio, and when people look at it, they say ''What — you write for THEM?'' which makes me really proud.'

5
Interviewing with Confidence

FINDING INTERVIEWEES

From neighbour's daughter to VIP

You can find interviewees living in your neighbourhood, or take their names and phone numbers from press releases. You may read a snippet about someone in a newspaper and decide it is worth expanding into a magazine feature.

Interviewees don't necessarily have to be famous. Anyone who does anything which could interest other people is worth interviewing. Many freelance journalists say that they could write at least one article about every new person they meet!

So who do you interview? Start with those close to you. Your sister, who is personnel manager for a large local company, about which job skills and qualifications are more in demand. Your brother-in-law, who works for a bank, about how to approach a bank manager for a loan. Your neighbour's daughter who has just won a local disco beauty contest. The author of a book which is to be launched soon and for which the publisher has sent you a press release. The rock group which consists of three students from the local college who've got a contract for their first single from a record company.

ARRANGING THE INTERVIEW

If you know the people personally, you can just ask them when you meet them next. Most 'normal' people are flattered to be interviewed; tell them honestly that you cannot guarantee publication.

Don't say you want to write an article about *them*. Say that you want to write about their work, their hobby, their charity, etc. Everyone enjoys talking about their work, but few like to talk about their private lives.

If potential interviewees are suggested by a press release, ring them up. They will probably ask for which publication you write. Mention the newspapers or magazines which have published your work before, and also to which editor you will be sending the interview. You must appear confident!

If you want to approach a VIP who has never heard of you, send a letter to him, or his agent or manager. They are unlikely to agree to be interviewed unless you can say that a particular editor has expressed interest, or unless you have had similar interviews published. (See Fig. 10, page 62.)

Your written request for an interview should suggest a date, a meeting place, the subject you want to talk about and the publication(s) for which the feature is intended.

You should give them a rough idea of the subjects you want to discuss during the interview, but avoid revealing the precise questions in advance otherwise you will end up with boring answers, carefully phrased by the public relations department.

When, where and how

The interviewee's office or home is the ideal meeting place. People are more relaxed in familiar surroundings.

It is tempting if an interviewee suggests meeting at a luxurious restaurant, especially if they offer to foot the bill. Once I interviewed a manager of an exclusive Swiss restaurant chain. But have you ever tried eating, talking and taking notes at the same time? While I tried to handle knife, fork and pen simultaneously, the delicious food got cold. And all I could hear when I played back the recorded tape was the noise of cutlery.

PREPARING FOR THE INTERVIEW

You don't need to be an expert on the chosen subject to make your interview a success. Experts who interview experts often lose touch with the uninformed reader's curiosity.

Ideally, you should know as little or as much as the typical reader of the magazine. If you interview a crime prevention officer for a women's magazine, you don't need any special knowledge. It does not matter if your questions are simple and naive — they are exactly the questions the readers want to ask!

Of course, the situation is different if you want to interview him for a police staff magazine. In this case you should know something about the subject, or your questions will seem naive.

Cathy Clever, Freelance Journalist
'Scribbles', 1 1 Abc Drive, Xyzzyx 1 YW WYA,
Tel & Fax: (0000) 0000
Member of the Society of Women Writers and Journalists

1 October 199x

Dear Amanda Amour,

I am a freelance journalist, writing for several newspapers and magazines. I am also a great fan of your films!

The press officer of Andromeda Films, André Anderson, has sent me a press release regarding your latest film, 'Autumn Affair'. I wonder if you would like to meet me for an interview.

Sabrina Sunday, the features editor of Suzanne Magazine, is interested in publishing it. I enclose a feature which has been published recently by the same magazine, to give you an idea of my writing.

The issues I would like to discuss are the different characters you represent in this and in your last film, how you prepare for a particular role, and how you enjoyed filming in Britain after three films made in Hollywood.

As you can see from my address, I live in your area, and could meet you either in your home or at any other place you suggest. I look forward to hearing from you.

Yours sincerely,

Cathy Clever

Cathy Clever

Fig. 10. Request for an interview.

It is vital that you establish yourself as a competent journalist. Wearing a suit will boost your confidence and create a professional atmosphere.

Have a list of questions ready when you go to the interview, arranged in the order you want to *ask* them. The order in which you want to write them up is irrelevant at this stage.

Using notebooks and tape recorders

A tape recorder is the most reliable recording method. It encourages the interviewee to talk faster and more spontaneously than if you take notes, and they cannot deny having said certain things afterwards! However, it can take up to eight hours to transcribe a one-hour recording.

Note-pads are convenient when it comes to writing up: paragraphs can be highlighted, cut out, rearranged, but unless your shorthand is fast you will lose details from the interview. I take notes of important comments and refer to the tape for detail.

HOW TO START AND HOW TO FINISH

The minutes before the actual interview are the most embarrassing; you will both feel better once the interview has started. Get straight into it, without chats about the weather.

Your interviewee's time — and yours — is precious. A well-prepared interview of 30 minutes provides ample material for a 1000-word feature. One hour should be the maximum if you have several markets in mind.

If your interviewee is nervous, put them at ease by asking simple questions which show that you appreciate what they are doing. Begin with a subject you know they enjoy talking about.

INTRODUCING INTERVIEWING TECHNIQUES

From gentle to cruel

Experienced journalists start with 'harmless' questions until the interviewee feels relaxed and safe. The critical subjects come later. One unwelcome question at the beginning may ruin the interview.

How to get the quotes you want

If you don't understand an answer, it is better to ask immediately than to phone up afterwards for clarification.

Questions about well-known facts are unwelcome. Imagine what the

Cathy Clever, Freelance Journalist
'Scribbles', 1 1 Abc Drive, Xyzzyx 1 YW WYA,
Tel & Fax: (0000) 0000
Member of the Society of Women Writers and Journalists

1 September 199x

Dear Madam or Sir,

I have been commissioned by Suzanne Magazine to write an article about male au pairs. Can you kindly assist me with my research by answering some or all of the questions in the enclosed questionnaire.

I am working to a tight deadline and would appreciate your reply by 10 October.

Publication is scheduled for spring next year, and I will send you a photocopy of the published article.

Thanks for your help. SAE enclosed.

Yours sincerely,

Cathy Clever

Fig. 11. Interview query.

famous actress will think of the journalist who asks, 'In which films have you played?'. Try 'Which film did you enjoy most? Why?'

If you agree with your interviewee's opinion, resist the temptation to say, 'Yes, I understand'. I have made this mistake, and realised afterwards that he would have continued talking if I had kept my mouth shut. I lost exactly *the* quote which I had been after.

Ask them for their opinions on everything. The stronger their views are, the better. These quotes will make your feature come alive.

Asking 'open questions' which cannot be answered with 'yes' or 'no' results in spontaneous answers which make splendid personality feature material. 'What were your impressions of filming in Paris?' invites a better answer than 'Did you like filming in Paris?'

Don't ever mention your own opinion. If you agree with your interviewee, the interview gets boring; if you disagree, you spoil the atmosphere, and either way you are wasting precious time.

Be flexible about an unexpected turn of story; some of your question ideas may turn out to be a dead end, while your journalist's instinct will suggest new angles.

COPING WITH FAMOUS, SHY OR DIFFICULT INTERVIEWEES

Most interviewees are helpful, proud to be interviewed or eager to impress the media.

If your interviewee is giving evasive answers in flowery words, he would prefer certain things not to come to light. Here is your story! Simply repeat the question, phrased differently, until he talks.

Some interviewees ask questions to test your knowledge and possibly undermine your self-confidence. Simply ignore them, even if you know an answer, and continue. You are the journalist, you ask and they answer.

Others give exciting information, adding 'But don't publish this.' You are not allowed to use any 'off the record' information. Say that you will respect their request, and keep your promise.

However, some interviewees make everything they tell you 'off the record', which means you cannot get enough information and quotes for a good feature. This can be because they are insecure, or because they want to appear mysterious and important. In this case you say: 'OK, if you have nothing to say to our readers, there is no point in me interviewing you.' They will become more helpful immediately!

Occasionally an interviewee tries to dictate the answers word by

Cathy Clever, Freelance Journalist
'Scribbles', 1 1 Abc Drive, Xyzzyx 1 YW WYA,
Tel & Fax: (0000) 0000
Member of the Society of Women Writers and Journalists

QUESTIONNAIRE

1. Do you accept male applicants for au pair jobs? If yes, do you think it is easier (or more difficult) for them to find a placement than for female au pairs? Why?

2. Do you get requests from families specifically for male au pairs? If yes, can you describe the typical family which employs a male au pair, and their reasons?

3. Do male au pairs, on average, do the same type of work as female au pairs, or are there differences? Which?

4. Are, in your experience, placements of male au pairs successful?

5. Can you possibly put me in touch with a family and their male au pair, so that I can interview them and take a photo of the au pair at work?

6. Do you believe that in future there will be more male au pairs? Why?

7. Any advice you want to give to boys who want to become au pairs?

8. Any other information you want to give?

Fig. 12. Questionnaire for interview by post.

word, including full stop and semicolon. Who do they think you are? The shorthand typist? Simply put away pen and pad, lean back comfortably in your chair and give them a wide smile. They will quickly treat you as a journalist!

TAKING PHOTOS

If you want to take photos do it after the interview, when the interviewee is relaxed and animated. Or take a photographer with you who can capture your interviewee in animated conversation, with gestures, facial expressions, etc and a photo captioned 'Actress Amanda Amour in discussion with journalist Cathy Clever'.

WRITING IT UP

Write the interview up soon, while you can still read your shorthand and your impressions are fresh. You will not be able to use all the interesting information you have, at least not in one article. Concentrate on one aspect for each publication.

It is alright to shorten answers, restructure sentences, drop repetitions, correct the grammar and rephrase certain answers so that they read better. However, don't be tempted to change the tiniest bit of the meaning, or you will be in deep trouble.

Most interviewees ask to see the feature before it goes into print. They will show it to their family, friends or PR consultants who will change everything completely. If they insist, offer to read it out to them on the telephone. They can then correct obvious misunderstandings, without a chance to consult anyone.

TELEPHONE INTERVIEWS

Once you are familiar with the basic interviewing techniques, you can conduct most interviews by telephone. This saves you a lot of travelling time and cost. Agree in advance a mutually convenient time, and also who will be phoning whom. Have a list of questions ready.

INTERVIEWS BY POST

These work well if it is not possible to meet the interviewees in person or to make telephone contact; for example, if you are interviewing a missionary in deepest Africa.

Interviews by post are also a time-saving device if you want to ask several people the same questions. Phrase your questions so that your interviewees can answer them in just a few sentences. Most of your questions must be 'open', otherwise your interviewees will simply say 'yes' or 'no' and you won't get any quotes. Photocopy the questionnaire, write a covering letter explaining the purpose of the survey, and give the date by which you need the reply and enclose a stamped addressed envelope. (See sample covering letter, Fig. 11, page 64 and sample questionnaire, Fig. 12, page 66.)

You can expect that eight out of ten people will respond.

A drawback of this method is that some interviewees reply in long, complicated sentences which don't read like natural talk, and others supply quotes which read like extracts from their sales literature.

WHAT THE EDITORS SAY

Ian Boughton, group editor of *Stationery Trade News,* encourages writers not to be afraid of interviewing experts: 'A very good tip to the aspiring freelance journalist is to remember that although you may not be a specialist in whatever subject you're writing about, you can find someone who is! There's nothing wrong with finding the source of wisdom and saying, quite openly, "I don't understand the situation — can you explain it in words of one syllable?" The chances are that the reply will give you your story, your angle, and your quotes as well.'

Alan Travell, editor of *Freelance Writing & Photography* and *Escape – The Career Change Magazine*: 'Sketch out some ideas for questions before you go to the interview, but don't look on them as a bible. Don't be pre-set in your thoughts. Be flexible, follow where the interviewee is going. What the interviewee has to say is more important and interesting than your preconceived ideas.'

Jill Stevens, community editor of the *Kent Messenger*: 'The most important thing, which many writers forget, is you have to listen! Many arrive at the interview armed with a list of questions, and as soon as one question has been answered, they write it down and move on to the next question on their list. They don't allow the interview to flow. Listen carefully, and your interviewees will reveal the unexpected.

'Another mistake for interviewers is to talk too much. You must remember: you are there just to prompt.'

6
Structuring and Writing the Feature

RESEARCHING

Depending on the type of article, and how much you know about your subject already, your research may include:

- A visit to your library, to borrow and order books and to look up reference works. If possible, make the most economical use of your time by researching for more than one feature at a time.

- Using press releases. As soon as you have had a few articles published on their subject, most organisations and companies will be happy to send you regular free information and the latest news, as well as interview ideas and even photos. Many press releases are waffling texts written in PR style, but they are valuable for ideas and contacts. (see Fig. 13, page 70 and Fig. 14, page 72.)

- Interviewing an expert.

- Interviewing other people, who hold a different opinion or who represent a different viewpoint.

DEVELOPING IDEAS INTO ARTICLES

You know exactly what you want to write about. You have researched the subject and the possible markets. And yet, you sit at your typewriter and just don't know how to get started. Professional journalists, staff or freelance, turn out reams of copy within tight deadlines. They have developed methods of writing articles on anything, without delay.

Some of the most brilliant features in the national newspapers and magazines are structured with the experienced journalist's standard formula. Using a tried and tested approach is a good way to get started.

Purple Panther Productions

Press release

Embargoed until: 11 November 199x

Jazz-punk group launches single

Oakhurst-based punk band Pink Poodles are launching their first single 'Paranoid Parachute' on 1 December 199x. Track A, 'Paranoia' is a mixture of soft rock and punk rock, with strong instrumental interludes. 'Parachute' on track B is a lively punk piece with traditional jazz elements.

The members of the band, Aaron Alberti (17, sax, lyrics), Bertie 'Bad' Brummer (21, percussionist and composer), and Coralie Corrall (18, guitar, vocals) are students at Oakhurst College.

All three are available for interview. For more information, photos, a review copy of the single or to arrange an interview, phone Paola Pomms on (0000) 00000.

Fig. 13. Press release (1).

USING AN INFALLIBLE FORMULA

Few journalists are willing to reveal their methods, but you can certainly try mine. Of course, you don't need to follow them strictly, and you can adjust them to suit your particular subject or market. I don't claim my guidelines are the only possible way to structure a feature, and they are not always the best. But I promise that they work, every time.

HOW TO WRITE A 'HOW TO' ARTICLE

'How to' articles are easy to sell and easy to write. Almost any subject can make a suitable 'how to' article, and almost everyone can give competent advice on one or more subjects. Articles which show, in the widest sense, how to earn or save money are bestsellers.

Before putting pen to paper, make sure you've 'done it' yourself. Most 'how to' articles are timeless and can be reslanted and sold to several publications. Study several target markets, and note the subjects, style and length of their 'how to' articles.

Use short words and sentences, avoid wordiness at all costs. Link words such as 'and then. . .', or 'after that', are superfluous. Always give precise measurements. 'Add half a teaspoonful of salt, and simmer for three minutes' is more helpful than 'Add a little salt and simmer for a while'. Be detailed without patronising the reader. Mention prices where appropriate.

This is the typical structure:

1. One introductory paragraph which motivates the reader.

2. Between three and twelve **bullet points** (or up to 20 numbered paragraphs) of one or two sentences. Arrange them in chronological order (what to do first).

3. The last paragraph should give sources of further information: further reading, addresses of mail order catalogues, courses and workshops.

Before sending out your manuscript, give it to a friend to read, to see if your instructions are clear and foolproof. If possible, ask your friend to try them out!

Fran's Frozen Foods

PRESS RELEASE

11 November 199x

Fran's pizzas are the best

Fran's are the most popular brand of frozen pizzas in East Sussex, according to an independent survey carried out by Frick's Data Services in October.

98.5% of a representative sample group of consumers aged 18 - 80 named Fran's Crispy Quark Pizza as their favourite in the '6" frozen pizza with crispy quark base and mushroom & tomato topping' category.

Product shots (b/w prints and trannies) are available. The managing director of Fran's Frozen Foods, Ms Francesca Firenze, is available for interview: Tel (000)) 00000.

Fig. 14. Press release (2).

WRITING THE INTERVIEW FEATURE

Personality profiles are based on interviews, and are always in demand. Bear in mind that quotes characterise a person better than description. Most beginners structure personality profiles like a CV in chronological order, which tends to be boring. Here's how to do it better.

1. Begin with a short, succinct quote which characterises the person's attitude to his/her work.

2. One sentence about the person, who he/she is.

3. One sentence which quantifies his/her recent success with a precise, surprising figure ('one million records sold').

4. One paragraph quote how he/she feels about this achievement, broken up by a description of his/her appearance, gestures, facial expression or tone of voice ('there is pride in her deep voice when she talks about. . .').

5. Continue alternating one or two paragraphs of narration with one paragraph of quote.

6. End with a humorous quote.

WRITING NEWS ARTICLES

The news articles must say who is doing what, where, when, how and why. Of these, the 'what' is the most important, and must be said in the first sentence. Avoid lengthy names (such as East Sussex County Council, or Citizen's Advice Bureau) in the first paragraph, because they put the reader off.

The who, what, where, when, how and why should be covered in the first two paragraphs. Many writers try to squeeze all the information into the first sentence, which results in constructions such as 'Citizens of Boarshurst are being urged by Ms Emma Louis, secretary of the local Save our River charity, to join a letter writing campaign which started last month and is intended to continue until September, by sending letters to the county council demanding in politely phrased requests that the decision to allow motor boats on our river should be reconsidered, to protect the wildlife in and around the section of the river between

Boarhurst and Crannington which would be endangered by the traffic of motor boats.' Better start with: 'Our river wildlife is in danger,' claims Ms Emma Louis. The secretary of the Save our River charity has started a campaign to prevent motor boats between Boarshurst and Crannington.' Then arrange the facts in order of importance.

When there is not enough space on the editorial page, editors have to cut news articles. This is done at the last minute, and there is no time to discuss the matter with the journalist who wrote the piece.

However, there is an unspoken agreement throughout the world of journalism that, if in doubt, subeditors will cut from the end. Don't leave the most important item to the last paragraph; it may be chopped off!

WRITING THE TOPICAL FEATURE

Many newspapers and magazines publish in-depth features to provide background information to news articles. The difficulty is that you have to obtain controversial quotes, and compile and verify a huge amount of information within a short time. If you can at the same time give the feature a new angle and show the facts in a different light, you deserve a byline in a national newspaper!

1. Start with one or two sentences describing the fact as it is generally seen.

2. One paragraph which shows the fact in a new light.

3. One paragraph quote by someone who is competent and well-known and who sees the facts in this light.

4. Two paragraphs analysing the background of the situation in more depth.

5. One-paragraph quotes from someone who holds a different opinion (probably your first contact's competitor or opponent, or the 'villain').

6. One paragraph quoting your first contact, contradicting what the second person said.

7. One paragraph narration.

8. One paragraph quote from a third person, such as the woman in the street.

9. Continue by alternating one or two paragraphs of narration, one paragraph of quote. As topical features usually cover unexpected events for which the editor has not planned space in advance, she will throw another piece out and fit the topical feature instead. This means that topical features often have to be cut drastically to fit into the available space. The same rule applies as for the news article: make sure that you give the essential bits in the first few paragraphs, and the less important information further down.

10. End with a paragraph which gives a summary and a critical (but not patronising or moralising) future outlook.

WRITING THE SUBJECT FEATURE

The typical subject feature is of a specialist nature (*eg* Hungary as a Developing Market for Ice Cream Exports), often long and in depth. Because of the wealth of information and the factual treatment, subject features tend to be boring to read. Do your best to liven them up with quotes.

1. Begin with an **intro** paragraph which may contain your byline ('Amanda Scribble visited Hungary to investigate the country's market potential'). This paragraph must contain a surprising fact, which is topical and of relevance to your feature, to hook the reader.

2. Begin the main text with a provocative quote from someone who is knowledgeable (perhaps the director of a company which exports ice cream to Hungary).

3. Write two paragraphs of explanation about the situation (why do so many western European producers target the Hungarian market? How much ice cream do Hungary's own factories produce?).

4. For the rest of the feature, alternate quotes and narration. Use quotes from several people who represent different viewpoints (another British producer eager to export, as well as the leader of a 'buy Hungarian' anti-import pressure group, a Hungarian housewife and mother of four, and an ice cream salesman).

For narrative, use hard facts ('The most popular flavours are chocolate, coffee and coconut'), backed up with figures ('total annual ice cream consumption is 1.7 litres per capita').

5. Keep your own opinion out. Instead, finish with a quote from someone competent who sums up the situation in the way you think, and who can give a brief statement of what to expect for the future.

WRITING THE CONTROVERSIAL FEATURE

This one is difficult both to write and to sell. Don't tackle it until you have some experience, and even then you should discuss the approach with the editor first.

Structure a controversial article or feature like a subject feature, and make sure that you give the two opposing parties equal space, but give the last word to the party with which most of your readers identify.

As subeditors cut from the end, don't write a huge chunk about party A and then a huge chunk about party B. The subeditor who is pressed for space may cut most of B's quotes. Use a pattern of one paragraph for A, one for B, and one for facts, and repeat this until the end of the feature.

WRITING THE OPINION FEATURE

Opinion features are the most popular category among beginner writers, but the least popular among the editors!

There are hardly any commercial outlets for opinion features, unless you are a VIP expert in your field. However, you can try writing a comment column for your club's or society's newsletter. Last but not least, the structuring recipe for opinion features is suitable for a reader's letter.

If you want to see it published, avoid the typical beginner's approach (opening with a well-known fact, with a proverb or a question) — this would read like a school essay! Avoid a patronising tone.

1. Start with a surprising fact, if possible relevant to the season or to a topical event, and develop your thoughts from there.

2. Alternate two sentences of thoughts, two sentences of facts,

throughout the feature. This makes your article easily readable. Quote a couple of precise figures and state the source; they make you appear competent.

3. Finish with a question, related to the future.

WRITING THE PERSONAL EXPERIENCE FEATURE

Never pretend to have tried something if you haven't, or your readers lose their trust in you. Take courage and try out that helicopter flight, hypnosis, or bungee jump. Mention your scare just before take-off, or how you almost changed your mind before jumping, and your readers will believe every word you say.

Start with a surprising fact or quote. Alternate narrative and quotes, facts and experience. Create atmosphere by describing noises and smells. Consider writing in the present tense for extra impact.

The best illustration is a picture of you in action, to prove that you've actually done it! Get a friend (or a professional from the newspaper's photographic department) to capture you in trance during hypnosis, or in full harness ready for the bungee jump.

WRITING A REGULAR COLUMN

Before suggesting a column to the editor, make sure you have plenty of ideas. Imagine you are having tea with the average reader: what would you talk about? You need not represent the average reader's opinion, as long as the subject is one which interests him. Editors appreciate columnists who receive bags of fan or hate mail. To stimulate the discussion, write about dog fouling, abortion or fox hunting. You can be sure the readers will write in.

A well-written column reads as if the author had written it in a careless, chatty tone, but it requires careful phrasing. Prune your manuscript until there is no superfluous word left.

DEVELOPING A GOOD WRITING STYLE

Every writer has her own style, and so has every magazine and newspaper, depending on the audience it wants to reach. The *Daily Mail*, for example, uses shorter sentences than *The Financial Times*.

Try to imitate the writing style of the publication for which you want to write as closely as possible. Pick out one or two typical articles and examine them closely. How many words do they use, on average, in a sentence? Out of one hundred words, how many words have more than one syllable?

How to make a subeditor happy

- As a general rule, try to keep your sentences below 25 words, and never exceed 33. Don't use a long word where there is a short one, and prefer Anglo-Saxon words to Latin ones.

- Use lots of expressive verbs, and keep adjectives and adverbs to a minimum.

- Ruthlessly cut all the following words out of your first draft: very, really, truly, totally, completely, absolutely, rather, quite, extremely. They are unnecessary. For example: 'He was quite disappointed that he did not get the job.' Either he was disappointed or he wasn't. 'The village was totally destroyed by the earthquake.' 'The good news made her really happy.' Watch out for 'very'; many freelances use this word in every sentence. You should not use it more than twice in a thousand words.

- Never use the word 'only' in connection with a price. State how much an item costs, and let the reader decide if it's cheap or expensive.

- Avoid PR speak, especially when quoting business people and when using extracts from press releases. 'High quality' is an over-used phrase, and can be replaced by the simple word 'good'. Words such as 'unique' and 'exceptional', popular with public relations people, are out of place in journalistic writing. If you describe the product, service, place or event properly, your reader will come to the conclusion that it is 'unique' if it truly is different from all others.

- Avoid empty words, such as 'interesting', 'nice', 'lovely', 'exciting', 'fascinating' and 'beautiful'. They pretend to describe something, but they don't. Choose words which give a more accurate description instead. Beauty is in the eye of the beholder, anyway.

- Avoid exclamation marks. Ideally, each of your sentences should be powerful enough to get your point across, without exclamation marks. The weaker the writing, the stronger the temptation to use exclamation marks. Two exclamation marks in a one thousand words text are acceptable.

Following the house style

Most publications have their own rules on grammar, spelling and the use of words. If you write regularly for a particular paper, ask for a copy of the house style notes.

These state whether it is the managing director, the Managing Director, the md, the MD, or the M.D. who gave the speech, whether Mrs Beech, Ms Beech or Diana Beech was elected, and whether she became chairman, chairwoman, chairperson or chair. They also decide the question of whether a phone number is written '(000) 000', '000 000' or '000-000'.

Not all potential questions are covered in the relevant editors' house style sheets. In this case, you must decide for yourself.

It is a good idea to set up your own house style, to which you refer whenever there is no other guidance available. This makes your writing consistent. It would look awkward if, in an article which contained lots of contact addresses, the telephone numbers were prefaced sometimes 'tel.', sometimes 'Tel:' and sometimes 'phone'.

Avoiding sexism

The use of 'he' and 'she' worries many writers. You don't want to be sexist, but you don't want your article to read like a legal document on equal opportunities either. You have the following possibilities:

1. You can use 'he', 'his' and 'him' throughout. Example: 'If a writer wants to sell his work, he must study his markets.' This is easy to read and easy to write, but it can prevent female readers from identifying with the article. It may even offend them. Another disadvantage is that it gives your writing a conventional, even old-fashioned flavour, and you add to the subconscious belief of many people that men form the majority of people and are more important than women. Choose this form if you write mostly for a conservative, exclusively male audience.

2. You can use 'she', 'hers' and 'her' throughout. Example: 'If a writer wants to sell her work, she must study her markets.' Again,

this is easy to read, but can prevent male readers from identifying and may offend them. It gives your writing a modern, even aggressive flavour. Choose this form if you write mostly for a female and feminist audience.

3. You can use 'she or he' (or 'he or she', 'she/he', 's/he' and so on) throughout. Examples: 'If a writer wants to sell her or his work, she or he must study his or her markets.' 'If a writer wants to sell his/her work, s/he must study his/her markets.' This form is certainly non-sexist and non-offensive, but it interrupts the flow and makes the article difficult to read. Choose this form if you write mostly short, factual articles.

4. You can use 'it' throughout, as some progressive writers suggest. Example: 'If a writer wants to sell its work, it must study its markets.' The idea is to abolish gender altogether, and with it any remains of sexual discrimination in writing. In practice, this doesn't work as well as in theory. For example, 'He gave it to her' becomes 'It gave it to it'. This can make it difficult for the reader to follow. Such a progressive approach would rarely endear your writing to the average editor.

5. You can use 'they', 'theirs' and 'them' throughout the article, even when referring to a single person. Example: 'If a writer wants to sell their work, they must study their market.' When this form was first introduced, some people were upset because it was grammatically wrong. However, it is short, practical, non-offensive, non-sexist, allows the text to flow and is easy to read. This has become the standard for many writers and many publications, and is becoming increasingly popular.

6. You can use 'he' for some paragraphs and 'she' for another. This gives your writing a real-life flavour and creates an effect as if you were using case studies. Both men and women can identify with your writing, and it is easy to read. This form is used frequently in America, and is becoming popular in Britain, too. However, it only works for books, long articles and features. If you switch from one gender to another within a sentence or a paragraph, or switch five times in a two-paragraph article, the result can be ridiculous.
    I have used this approach for much of this book.

Of course, if a publication's house style requires a particular way of dealing with 'he' and 'she' then you must follow it, whatever your own house style and opinion is.

WHAT THE EDITORS SAY

- Ian Boughton, group editor of *Stationery Trade News* and other publications, advises: 'Find the angle. I know this is basic page-one-diagram-three stuff, but too many of the freelance pieces I see have been written in school essay style (start at the beginning and go through the facts in chronological order, then finish).

  'I promise that the basic tactic of finding the angle and highlighting it in a decent paragraph will work just as well on the editor as it will on the reader. If you inspire a ''fancy that!'' reaction, you've caught their attention.'

- Diana K Jones, editor of *The Disabled Driver*, says: 'Stick to the subject. For news articles, give instant impact. For features, develop interest and growth. Interest your readers from the beginning. Grab and hold on to that interest.'

- Alan Travell, editor of *Escape* and *Freelance Writing & Photography*: 'You must grab the audience from the beginning. If I like the first few sentences, I'll read to the end. A mistake frequently made by writers is writing in a patronising style, talking down to the readers. This does raise my hackles a bit.'

- Jill Stevens, community editor of the *Kent Messenger*: 'When contributing articles to newspapers, the important rule is to keep it short. Editors are taking far more kindly to short articles than to a long one, which they may not even bother to read. A news article must cover the Who What When Where Why. Remember that news is what is happening today but did not happen yesterday. Put the important information in the intro, and a contact name at the bottom.'

7
Branching Out

WRITING ADVERTISING FEATURES

Do you read the advertising features in your local newspaper? Perhaps not. You find them boring, predictable, with more flowery phrases than entertainment value or information. You don't want to read about yet another business and its 'commitment to quality', about how it 'achieves highest standards' because 'customer satisfaction' comes first for its 'friendly, helpful staff' who are 'always at hand'.

The advertisers, of course, are flattered to see themselves praised in print. They are happy if their services are described as 'delightful', 'fascinating', 'exciting', 'interesting' and 'unique'.

A good advertising feature, however, does more than flatter the advertiser. It captures the readers' attention, gains their trust, informs and entertains them. In short: it brings customers for the business.

Attention, interest, desire, action

Do you know AIDA? Not Verdi's opera, but the formula to which skilled marketing people work. It is their recipe for a successful advertising campaign. You can apply it to creating advertising features, or advertorials as they are sometimes called.

- A stands for **attention**. You have to make the readers look at your feature, so arouse their curiosity at first sight. Most ad features fail at this point already.

  Faced with a huge choice of tempting headings on the news pages (Sex at The Bus Stop, Sonya Challenges The Football Star, Ex-Mayor Jailed, who is going to be attracted by typical adfeat headings such as Experienced and Polite Staff Are Always at Hand, and Where Quality and Customer Satisfaction Come First?

  And with all the photos of little children, cuddly dogs, TV stars and page-three girls, who is going to waste a second glance on the portrait of a middle-aged man in suit and tie?

The average readers pick just what springs to their eye immediately, and discard the rest unread. You have only a few seconds to capture their attention.

- I for **interest**. Make your intro paragraph so interesting that they want to find out more.

- D stands for **desire**. Make them want the product. Most adfeat writers exaggerate the desirability of the product so much that the reader does not believe them, over-using PR words such as 'exciting' and 'delightful'. Be honest with your readers, and they will believe you and your recommendation.

- A is for **action**. Stimulate the readers to go and spend money on the product. Here, too, most adfeat writers go too far, pushing the readers into purchasing action. 'So on your next free evening, go and visit the Pin and Needle Restaurant. . .'.

  Your readers feel patronised if you try to force the decision on them, particularly if you say that a three course meal costs 'only £57 per head'. State the prices, but leave it to the reader to decide if it is 'only' or 'just'. What seems a reasonable price to you may be unaffordable to a single mother or an unemployed worker. 'Only £9.99' intimidates them. Allow them to relax, to form their own opinion, and they may make their own decision to go and try out the meal.

I find that most adfeat writers ignore A (attention) and I (interest), thus losing most potential customers. Then they exaggerate D (desire) and A (action), bore most of their readers and intimidate the rest.

More than praise in print
Can you do better? Why not try your hand at an advertising feature, just to find out? Write about a friend's or neighbour's business. If you like the result, you can show it as a sample of your work to your local newspaper. Many papers have no money for freelance reporters and fiction writers, but there is almost always a budget for advertising features.

Advertising features are also called 'advertorials', 'editorial promotion' or whatever name the advertising department has invented.

Instead of the predictable litany of company praise, try any of the following approaches.

Personality profile

Base it on an interview with the owner (see page 73). This version is the easiest to write, and the most interesting to read. Give it a lot of human touch, which will make the reader remember the person (and her or his business) for months. Instead of the usual head and shoulders full-front portrait, take a photo of the person at work.

Personal experience feature

This means great fun during the research, and a chance to get a **freebie**, too. See page 77 on how to write the personal experience feature.

Company history

This is popular with companies celebrating an anniversary. It works well if the company is at least 100 years old, if you can use old photos and if there are plenty of anecdotes. Readers are not interested in who succeeded whom as chairman: they want to read the funny bits.

Obtain old photos from the company's archives, if possible with people. Then take your own photo of the same venue or equivalent situation. This makes eye-catching 'now' and 'then' pictures.

Trend survey

This is difficult to write for a beginner. Have a few questions ready: Who are your youngest customers? Your oldest? Do people of different age groups have different tastes? Do men select different products from women? Do they know what they want, or do they require advice? Which product is particularly popular with price conscious consumers? Which colour/style/size, etc is in at present? Do couples take the decision together . . . or is it the man/the woman who decides? Photo suggestion: manager or staff demonstrating the most popular product to customers.

Staff round-up

Take photos of several members of staff at work. Select staff who are working at different levels and in different departments, *eg* saleswoman, receptionist, manager. Give preference to people who have been with the company for many years, and whom your readers are likely to meet. Describe their daily work, their responsibilities, and how they contribute to the finished product. Use their quotes to liven up the text.

HOW TO WRITE A PRODUCT TEST COLUMN

You are honest and diplomatic at the same time. You enjoy trying out new things, have a vivid imagination and can use words creatively. Then writing a product test column could be your strength!

Many newspapers, trade and consumer magazines carry such columns, in which someone gives a subjective view. Products tested include, depending on the publication, everything from lipstick to cars, from wine to sports equipment, from pens to holidays.

Rates vary enormously; they can be nominal or substantial. In some cases there is no payment at all — but the 'freebies', *ie* the free products, make up for it.

Once you've decided which type of product you are going to test, you write to the press departments of the producers to request a sample. They are usually keen to have their products reviewed, but first you must convince them that you are a bona fide journalist and that your product tests will get published. Send a photocopy of your press card, of your Society of Women Writers and Journalists membership card, or whatever credentials you have. Better still, enclose a sample of a previously published product review.

The easiest way to break into product testing is possibly to write for your local paper, if necessary without payment at first. They often request a local angle for all features. You can achieve this by simply including the names of stockists in the area.

Specify precisely the product you are testing: 'mascara, waterproof, black', or 'night cream for ageing skin'. You need between three and twelve products for a proper test column.

Make sure you give each a fair trial — for example don't test the duration of one lipstick during a theatre performance and the other during dinner or while making love! To test nail varnish apply the ten different products at the same time, one on each nail, so that they are exposed to the same amount of nail biting and washing up.

Finding the right words

Ignore the flowery phrases of the press releases which arrive with the products. 'This exquisite moisturiser is perfectly balanced and uniquely suited for today's busy lifestyle. . .'. Find your own descriptions, based on your experience. They will necessarily be subjective, which is alright for an opinion column. Plain language is best, but you may use colourful metaphors and comparisons. Say what the product looks, smells, feels like.

Use comparisons with which your readers are familiar and which mean the same to them as they mean to you. Wine journalists, for example, tend to use words like 'biscuity' or 'hint of vegetable', and leave their readers wondering if the wine tastes of rich tea or chocolate biscuits, of broccoli or asparagus!

Be critical. If you find fault with a product, you owe it to your readers to be honest. But make sure that you say something positive as well. 'This cream had a wonderfully fresh fragrance which reminded me of peaches, but after one hour my skin felt tight and itchy.' Or: 'Despite three coatings, this nail varnish lasted only one day. But it was easy to apply and dried quickly.'

State the name of the product and the manufacturer precisely, as well as the quantity and — important — the recommended retail price.

Accepting 'freebies'

Once you are established as a journalist in your field, especially if your writing includes product tests, you will be wooed by manufacturers and their public relations consultants.

Will you remain unbiased if a cosmetic producer sends you the whole range of autumn colours to test for your beauty column? If you are among the lucky handful of travel writers who get invited to foreign press trips, will you give the sponsoring travel organiser the same treatment as others? Be as honest as you possibly can. It is alright to:

- Accept small gifts which have no great commercial value, on such occasion as Christmas, a press reception or a product launch.

- Accept an invitation for a meal.

- Accept samples of products which help you do your research (for example, if you are a beauty columnist, a lipstick in the latest shade, or if you are a wine writer, a bottle of wine).

- Accept travel expenses to visit a factory or attend a product launch. However, it is rare for companies to offer to refund travel expenses, so don't rely on it.

- Ask for samples, free admission to theatres and exhibitions, review copies of books and records and so on if you are certain that you will write about them, and confident that you will get the article published.

- Send a thank you note to companies which have sent you samples or gifts.

- Write more about companies which have been helpful with your research and allowed you to sample their products, than about those who have even ignored your request for a brochure.

- Send photocopies of articles which mention products and services to the relevant companies.

However, you must not:

- Accept valuable gifts which have nothing to do with the subject you write about.

- Accept gifts where the quantity is out of proportion to what you are doing. For example, if you are writing a feature about champagnes, you don't need a whole case of each vintage.

- Accept anything with the promise or unspoken understanding that you will praise a product or service in return.

- Put your own interests (continuing supply of free samples) before your readers' interests (objective reporting).

- Penalise companies which don't send samples by writing negative comments about them.

- Ask for samples if you are unlikely to write about the products or services. Begging letters from false 'travel journalists' requesting free accommodation are an example.

- Accept cash (except for travel expenses).

- Sell products you are given for research.

WRITING ABOUT TRAVEL

Many journalists dream about being a travel writer, touring the world at somebody else's expense and writing an article now and then. The market is competitive, and it's hard to make a living. Even if you find a sponsor for your trip to Florida and a newspaper to buy your articles at a rate of £100/1000, you cannot fit more than a couple of two-week trips into a month, which means you won't earn more than £200 per month.

Few journalists make a living from travel writing. Others specialise in other subjects and do occasional travel writing to finance their holidays.

How to write a travel feature

Articles about exotic places untouched by westerners, and about your immediate neighbourhood, both sell well, provided you come up with an unusual angle. For a travel article it is alright to use the first person approach and tell the story of your personal experience.

Avoid boring starts ('Middleham in Yorkshire is a popular holiday destination'), and don't open the article before your arrival ('My husband and I studied many travel brochures, considering numerous destinations, before deciding on Middleham in Yorkshire'). Open with a bang, with a surprising fact ('seven hundred and eighty-four people, four hundred race horses and eight ghosts live in Middleham') or a startling or funny quote ('We don't eat horse meat here in Middleham. It would be an expensive meal, at 100,000 guineas for each of the race horses').

A good travel feature entertains first and informs second. Talk to the locals, and include their quotes, as well as personal anecdotes. Weave the facts unobtrusively between the lines of your article, or put them into a separate **box** at the end of the manuscript.

Mike Gerrard, a professional travel journalist, advises: 'Keeping notes is vital, even if you use only ten per cent of them. You never know in advance which bits you are going to use. Always jot down your immediate reaction.'

Use all your senses. A brief description of a smell gives a much clearer impression of a place than several paragraphs describing the view.

Mike Gerrard also suggests that you 'write more about less. Don't try to cover a region's history, markets, beaches, museums, people and traditions in a single article, or you will not have room to write anything in detail. Instead elaborate on things. Concentrate on one market, or one festival.'

Finding out more

Mike Gerrard gives weekend and one-week courses in journalism. He has also written and published a booklet about travel writing, which is available for £1.50 plus postage. For his address, and other organisers of travel writing courses, see Useful Addresses, page 157.

Daily newspapers, such as *The Guardian, The Times, The Independent* and *The Daily Telegraph* publish travel sections on Saturdays, and they consider unsolicited features although the chances of acceptance are small. Other markets include women's magazines, which are particularly interested in the sex lives of women in other countries, and travel magazines, such as *Traveller* and *Wanderlust* which have detailed guidelines for contributors (send sae).

WRITING REVIEWS

When reviewing a book, a play, a film or an exhibition, you should give your personal impression as well as some facts.

If it is the work of amateurs, mention as many names as possible. They will be delighted to see their names in the paper. Be generous with praise, and careful with criticism.

When you are reviewing the work of professionals, on the other hand, you can be frank. You are not obliged to recommend a play just because the theatre gave you free tickets. However, readers prefer reading positive reports. You should always mention some positive aspects as well. If you feel there is nothing positive to say whatsoever, contact your editor. He may decide to publish your piece nevertheless, or he may decide that as the subject was so terrible, it doesn't deserve a mention at all.

Read review columns by other writers and learn how they handle the delicate task of criticising. A diplomatic strategy is to say for whom the reviewed work is suitable: 'If you enjoy crude jokes, you will love this play. Those who prefer subtle humour may be disappointed.'

CASE STUDIES

Matt

'I'm doing test drives for the local paper, borrowing the latest cars from the local garages, and the manufacturers pay for the petrol. At first I didn't know what to write, and copied the information from the brochure, but the editor didn't like this approach.

'One Saturday I helped my mother with her shopping. She commented on how easy it was to load the shopping into the boot and to squeeze the car into the tiny parking space outside the supermarket. I quoted her. The garage manager told me that because of this article several women had come to see the car. I knew I was on the right track then.'

Cathy

'I'm writing a test column for the local newspaper. It has become popular with readers, so the editor asked me to continue. I'm trying out products suitable for families with children. At first I wrote about products I had bought, but now I get free samples from manufacturers and shops. My husband and children enjoy the testing, and I use their comments as quotes.

'A local toy shop says that sales of reviewed products have soared. Mind you, I've had a couple of nasty letters from manufacturers whose products were of poor quality.

'I also sent an article about our holidays, with the angle ''travelling with a handicapped child'' to a magazine, and it was accepted. Then I interviewed families with handicapped children about their travelling experiences, and sold the article to another magazine. I think I will specialise in this subject.'

Nigel

'Whenever a DIY shop, a plumber or a similar business wants an advertising feature, the editor of the local newspaper calls me. I get £20 per advertising feature, plus expenses.'

Joan

'I was sure that my travel feature about my once-in-a-lifetime trip to Tanzania would sell, but it has been rejected. Then I wrote a piece about where the BBC has made a film locally, visiting all the locations and interviewing some of the local extras, and the first editor I queried commissioned it. He said it was topical, and they didn't get enough travel pieces about places in the UK.'

8
Making the Big Money

TAPPING THE BEST PAYING MARKETS

Some publications pay as little as £2.50 per 1000 words, others pay £25 or £250. A small fee can be a great reward for the hobby journalist who writes for fun, and for the beginner who is eager to build a portfolio of published work. But once you've entered phase 3 (see page 20), or are aiming towards semi-professional or professional status (phases 4 and 5), you will concentrate on those markets which offer good or excellent rates.

Of course they are more demanding than your local paper or club newsletter, but by now you are an experienced writer. You have developed the writing and marketing skills which make a good journalist. For an experienced writer, breaking into the top-paying markets is as difficult or as easy as it is for a beginner to get a letter published in the local newspaper.

You have mastered one — there's no reason why you should not succeed with the other. Below are some examples which will give you an idea.

Among the publications which pay a good fee (£50-£100 per 1000 words) are:

- The lower circulation national women's magazines, such as *Woman Alive, The Lady*.

- Magazines targeted at a specific group of society, such as *Active Life, Disability Now, Eastern Eye*.

- Special interest publications which have a wide but limited readership, such as *Jobs International, Overseas Jobs Express, Practical Photography*.

- Trade magazines, such as *European Frozen Food Buyer, Your Business.*

Among the top-paying publications (£100-£400 per 1000 words) are:

- National newspapers. Payment is a matter of negotiation, but you can expect a fee in excess of £120/1000 words. If you are considered to be an expert in your subject, and if you have had features published in other prestigious publications, you will earn more.

- The 'big' women's magazines: *Company* pays £200/1000 words.

- High circulation trade magazines: *Retail Week* pays £120/1000 words.

- High circulation special interest magazines: *Car* pays £260/1000 words, *Computer Weekly* pays £150/1000 words.

- Business magazines: *Business Life* pays £300/1000 words. *Euromoney* pays £250/1000 words. *Marketing Week* pays £150/1000 words.

Of course, a change in editor or in editorial policy can mean a change in rates of pay, and in most cases payment is 'by arrangement'. But the above examples can give you an idea of what to ask for when negotiating your fee. More publications and their rates are covered in *The Writers' and Artists' Yearbook.*

WRITING FOR WOMEN'S MAGAZINES

No women's magazine is exactly like the others. Although a good idea may be suitable for several of them, the treatment must be different. Editors get annoyed if writers assume that one woman is like another, and that one women's magazine is like another. Why does one woman buy *Bella*, while others buy *Seventeen* or *Marie Claire*?

The most important factor is the age group. For example, if you write a feature about people who underwent a sex change, you must choose interviewees who are the same age as the readers. For example, 18-30 for *Company*, and 35 upwards for *Women's Journal.*

Consider their average income, too. For a feature on how to buy a second-hand car, think carefully if you choose a Porsche or a Fiat Panda as an example.

Other considerations are whether the average reader has children, whether she has a career, and if she is more domestic or outward oriented.

Remember that most women's magazines are keen to buy features which are sex- or money-oriented. Approach your subject accordingly.

The major features are almost always commissioned work, but fillers are often unsolicited material. Some women's magazines state categorically 'No unsolicited manuscripts'. Don't let this put you off. It doesn't mean that they are not using freelance material at all. Send in feature suggestions instead; if the editor says 'Well, maybe. I'd like to see this feature, send it on spec' it is no longer unsolicited.

If editors think of commissioning you to write a feature, they will ask for samples of your work. Send something which is as similar to the magazine's style as possible.

WRITING FOR TRADE AND BUSINESS MAGAZINES

The advantage of writing for trade magazines is that you have little competition. Trade magazine editors are not usually inundated with unsolicited manuscripts. They welcome contributions which are specifically aimed at their readers.

However, it can be difficult to understand the magazine's editorial requirements. If possible talk to a typical reader, for example a frozen food buyer if you want to write for *European Frozen Food Buyer*.

Study one issue in depth. Ask the editor or the distribution department to send you an out-of-date or damaged copy, or pay for a new issue. Many trade magazines have guidelines for contributors.

When I was acting editor of *European Frozen Food Buyer*, and deputy editor of *European Drinks Buyer*, I wrote detailed editorial guidelines explaining the angle, length and style I wanted. I even included suggestions for features I would like to see.

To my surprise most aspiring contributors, even after studying the guidelines, sent in pieces such as A Holiday in Iceland (perhaps she thought 'ice' was a sufficient connection with 'frozen'), and The History of Mineral Water.

Others took the guidelines seriously, and came up with several suggestions which were 'near misses'. In this case I explained where they went wrong, and asked for more ideas. Most of them became regular contributors.

Remember that trade magazines are business-oriented. The readers want to know how they can do better business, and how to save and earn more money.

Don't be discouraged if you don't know anything about frozen food, the stationery trade, window manufacture or retailing. What counts is that you are willing to take an interest in the subject.

Start by interviewing and writing about the people who are experts. After a few interviews you will be amazed how much you have learned about the subject. Of course it takes some time to get into a subject, so it is best to concentrate on one or two subjects and become an expert in them, rather than trying a bit here and a bit there.

'We on the trade or business-to-business press get fairly warlike at the idea that the trade press is where you go if you're not good enough for a daily,' says Ian Boughton of *Stationery Trade News*. 'I've seen it several times in the ''teach yourself'' kind of book, and from well-meaning lecturers and the like: the same old advice that the trade press is a good place to start off and get some experience.

'Drivel! We prefer to say that the dailies are where you go if you're not experienced enough for the trade press. . .'

Writing about business and finance is one of the most lucrative areas of journalism. If you are interested in business, it's worth learning about the subject, for example by reading business publications and by interviewing business people.

Tips for interviewing business people

The first interview with a business person can be daunting, especially if you know little about the subject and fear that you might make a fool of yourself. Here are a few tips, as well as questions which are suitable for almost any type of business:

1. Remember that you don't have to be an expert to interview an expert.

2. When interviewees mention figures ('our sales have increased by eighteen per cent over the last year'), ask what these figures refer to. Is your interviewee talking about UK, European or worldwide sales? Is he referring to sales in volume, or sales in value? If sales have increased in volume only, the company may be making less profit than the year before; perhaps they had to reduce prices to undercut their competitors. If sales have increased in value only, the company may be selling fewer products than the year before; perhaps they simply increased their prices.

3. Don't accept PR-speak from your interviewee. Everyone will try to tell you that their product offers 'excellent value for money' and is of the 'highest possible quality'.

4. Ask who their target consumer is. If your interviewee claims that the product is suitable for everyone, insist on details. Every product is designed with a specific consumer in mind. Ask for the socio-economic group, the age group, the gender and so on.

5. Ask how consumer behaviour has changed over recent years.

6. Ask how your interviewee expects consumer behaviour and demand for the product to develop over the next five years. He will predict increasing demand for the product. Keep asking for details.

7. Ask what influence the European Union has had on the business.

8. Ask if, and how, developments in Eastern Europe are influencing the market. Increased competition? Any plans for import, export?

SELLING AND RE-SELLING YOUR WORK

To make the big money, you must use your research and writing time efficiently. If you sell ten different articles based on one subject, you can cut down your research time to one-tenth. This gives you the time to research, write and sell even more articles. It increases your output and your income.

Can I sell the same article twice?

It is possible to sell a feature more than once, as long as you sold first British serial rights (FBSR) only. You can offer, for example, second British serial rights, or first Italian rights. State on your manuscript, or in the accompanying letter, where the article was published originally.

You can sell the article several times, as long as these publications are non-competing. A piece on how to become a bilingual secretary in France, based on an interview with three enthusiastic young women, could be published in a young women's magazine, in a magazine for secretaries and PAs, in *Overseas Jobs Express* and again in *Escape — The Career Change Magazine*.

You may have to make minor changes. For example, for the young women's magazine you will insert a couple of quotes on the glamorous lifestyle in Paris. For *Escape* you will use more quotes from the 18-year-old. You will also include details of what they did before they went abroad.

For the secretarial magazine you may add information on the equipment they are using, and for *Overseas Jobs Express* you explain in depth how they found their jobs.

SELLING ABROAD

Think European

As the European countries co-operate more closely in more areas than ever, the need for information from and about our neighbour states is increasing rapidly. You will have noticed how much editorial space in newspapers and magazines has been dedicated to European subjects.

At the same time, readers and editors in other European countries are eager to learn about what is going on in the UK. This situation offers a great chance for freelance journalists. When I was deputy editor of a business magazine with European readership, I was often approached by editors from other countries, asking if I could recommend a freelance business journalist in Britain.

Writing for foreign markets can be very profitable. This does not mean, however, that it is easier to sell work abroad than in your own country. Editors in Sweden or Luxembourg receive the same amount of unsolicited and unwanted manuscripts as their UK counterparts.

If you want to enter a niche market in Europe, you need to know how to approach foreign editors and what type of manuscripts they really want.

Real demand exists for the following categories: business and technical features, personality features, news articles.

Business and technical features

Many new European and worldwide publications have been launched recently. You will find their titles and addresses in *Willings Press Guide* or *Benn's Media Directory* in your reference library.

Watch out for titles beginning 'European. . .', 'Europäische. . .' etc. Most of them are specialist or trade publications, keen to find contributors outside their own country, and they are paying good rates. Technical, financial, computing and business magazines are the best paying publications.

Background knowledge in the relevant industry sector (such as advertising, food and drink, or rubber processing) is highly desirable. However, a keen interest in the subject, plus the ability to learn quickly and make contacts with knowledgeable people, is more important.

If you specialise in one subject, you will be able to write about what is going on in this sector in the UK market for a dozen publications in various European countries.

Some magazines are published in English; others are willing to sub a contributor's broken French, or to translate news articles into Spanish, provided the contents are what they want.

Personality features

Few features editors are willing to go to the trouble of translating and publishing a feature from a foreign contributor if it could be written by one of their native, regular freelances. Most general interest and how-to features fall into this category.

However, there is considerable demand for personality features. If you have a chance to interview a VIP, who is internationally known and based in your country, regard it as potential foreign markets material. Profiles of an opera singer, a football star, or a politician can be published in five or ten different countries at once.

News articles

Consider becoming the UK correspondent for a newspaper on the continent, particularly if you live in or near London and are interested in economic and political issues.

The biggest national dailies abroad have their own fully-staffed offices in London, but many medium-sized newspapers cannot afford a full-time journalist in every European capital. They are eager to find writers who can supply them with news and features on a regular basis. During the summer months, when very little happens in politics, the international news editors in all countries are desperate to fill their pages. Short features on environmental, social and cultural issues are welcome.

How to approach foreign markets

In addition to checking out titles and their contents in *Willings* and *Benn's*, you can explore foreign markets by buying foreign general interest, women's and business magazines at major newsagents in the UK, although they are usually expensive.

Whatever their language, it is possible to learn from their advertisements and illustrations at which audience, age and social group they are targeted, and to see how long their features are.

Bear in mind, however, that general interest and women's magazines are less keen on foreign contributions than the specialist publications.

You can approach overseas agencies in the countries of your choice. If you are a specialist in a certain subject, perhaps environmental or religious affairs, the national news agencies such as the German DPA (Deutsche Presse-Agentur) may be interested in your news articles. To maintain the news value you have to submit them by fax.

In some countries rates for freelances are much higher than in the UK. Denmark and Sweden, for instance, are lucrative markets. Southern and Eastern European publications usually pay less.

Remember to sell British rights only to your UK publisher. Then there is nothing to stop you from enjoying a supplementary income from European publications.

Using international syndication

If personality or travel features are your speciality, approach a **syndication** agent. Agents have contacts in many countries and may sell your features a dozen times. They charge 50 per cent of the fees you earn from them, but they pay for the postage abroad, for necessary translations and so on. You simply send them a photocopy of your published article, or of the manuscript.

Syndication agents prefer features which are of interest to readers in many countries. They don't want 'How the local government reorganisation affects East Sussex villages', but they are interested in an interview with a well-known concert pianist. Personality profiles and interview features are popular with syndication agents.

Photos help them sell your work. To persuade syndication agents to take you on, you have to convince them that you can send features in bulk — a dozen per month, if possible.

You find syndication agents, their addresses and the material they are looking for in the *Writers' and Artists' Yearbook*.

CASE STUDIES

Matt

'I enjoy watching motor racing. I live not far from Brands Hatch, and whenever there's an important race I try to interview as many drivers as possible. At first, I published them in the local newspaper, but then I landed some in the big magazines. Whenever a driver is known internationally I send the interview to a syndication agent, who sells it in Australia, New Zealand, Canada and other English-speaking countries. I have become their expert on motor racing.'

Cathy

'After having a couple of features accepted on travelling with disabled children, I interviewed a blind pianist. I sold this piece to a women's magazine. On the strength of this feature I was then commissioned to write one about a disabled designer. It seems there is a market for profiles of disabled VIPs. I approached a syndication agent, who liked the articles but said he would not take me on unless I could submit at least one manuscript per week. I will approach him again in a year or so.'

Nigel

'I'm writing for several trade magazines abroad: news, interviews, what's going on in the trade in Britain. It was difficult to get into these markets at first, but now I'm contributing regularly. Some of them pay very well, but others don't and it's difficult to chase up overdue cheques abroad. However, British editors are always impressed when they see that my features on the same subject have been published abroad. In this way, my foreign features increase my sales in the UK.'

Joan

'I offered a feature about women in Tanzania to the editor of a women's magazine. She phoned and asked me if I could write about their sex lives. I could not. I talked to so many women in Tanzania about so many subjects, but not about sex. Now I know. Next time I go abroad, I know what to research.'

WHAT THE EDITORS SAY

● Ian Boughton, group editor of *Stationery Trade News* and other trade publications, feels strongly about what makes a good freelance contribution and what doesn't. He advises aspiring contributors: 'When writing for the trade press you must show respect for the subject. I'm currently editing for the stationery and office-supplies industry, and I get no end of freelances thinking that this subject must be some silly little sector to do with rubber bands. Yet commercial stationery is worth £3 *billion* a year in Britain, and people have bought Jaguars, Rolls-Royces and big houses out of it.

I can tell you that one of the most breathtaking technological inventions I saw last year, which left me speechless, was something brilliant applied to the elastic band.

'Freelances must acknowledge that all subjects are serious to someone, and respect them. I expect the same applies everywhere from brass bands to dog food.

'You aren't going to believe this, which I swear is not just true, but has happened to me on several occasions. Working for a specific industry, we need our material to be trade-relevant. I have on many occasions made a point of saying to writers: "The piece *must* be trade-specific to our readers." "Oh yes", they say . . . and what happens? They merely insert an appropriate term at a dozen points in a general feature. For example, when writing about office-supplies, they just pop in the words "the stationer" here and there.

'Even worse, and I can offer this with a solid-gold guarantee of truth, I have had text submitted in which the writer has every so often crossed out references to, say, "the builder's merchant", and has written above it: "the stationer". Would you believe it?'

- Hilary Robinson, features editor of *Good Housekeeping*, explains what type of journalist is most likely to succeed in the women's magazines market: 'The ideal writers are imaginative and logical at the same time, intelligent with a dash of humour, and able to produce great writing. When it comes to commissioned work, they are honest about whether they want to do the piece.'

9
Building a Good Relationship with Your Editor

Most of your contact with editorial staff will be in writing, some in person and some over the phone. Whenever you meet, write or ring your editor, prepare what you want to say and try to get the right image across. Concentrate on being friendly, cheerful, helpful, professional, honest and efficient.

PRESENTING A MANUSCRIPT

Many freelances believe that editors decide about acceptance of a manuscript according to its outer appearance. 'How to write' books and magazines create an image of editors who always have a ruler at hand, and anything with less than 1.5" margins automatically lands on the rejection pile. However, these books and magazines are usually written by freelances, who have never worked on the editorial side!

In reality, editors buy contents, not presentation.

Before you cry out in protest because your creative writing tutor has told you otherwise: yes, I have worked as a magazine and newspaper editor; yes, I have published manuscripts which arrived as hardly legible, pale print outs on flimsy, dog-eared sheets. So have many other editors, particularly on specialist publications.

Remember, however, that the reason why editors buy freelance material is to save time.

Sloppy presentation costs time during editorial production, and only a unique feature will be considered worth the trouble.

A clean, legible manuscript saves time for the subeditor and the typesetter and is greatly appreciated.

Basic rules
The standard rules for manuscript submission are simple:

- typed (handwritten work will not even be looked at, except for readers' letters)

The call of the Wild Swans

Travel feature by Christine Hall
1000 words, FBSR

"You must not sleep now," warned Mr Bao, my host and guide. "There are highwaymen in this area, and they stop and rob cars like ours. Stay awake."

We had left the area of Beijing with its asphalt roads, lorries, bicycles, tricycles, horse and ox carts thirty hours ago. The car was creeping up the steep mountains of the Jilin Province in northeast China, on roads covered in mud and ice. It was getting dark and chilly.

Mr Bao did not tell me what to do should we be confronted by highwaymen, but he was worried about his car, the status symbol of his new wealth, with gold coloured upholstery and white lace headrests and curtains. The once poor English teacher has become a rich businessman.

He had promised a "fully furnished apartment with central heating and running hot water" for my stay. But when I arrived, cold and stiff from the long journey, I found the rooms bare, with broken window panes, defective wiring, sporadic periods of heating and no water supplies at all, while a blizzard was raging outside. "I am a busy man," Mr Bao shrugged. "You cannot expect me to keep all my promises."

These are the drawbacks of a tour "off the beaten track" in a remote area which is virtually untouched by tourism.

Having read Jung Chang's book "Wild Swans", which tells the story of three generations of Chinese women – from the concubine of a warlord to a language student who is not allowed to use her English – I was determined to find out how the women in the former Manchuria live today.

Fig. 15. First page of a manuscript.

- double-spaced (for easy reading, corrections and changes by the editorial staff)

- margins on both sides (again for corrections; normal correspondence margins are alright)

- on white A4 paper, typed on one side only (you can use a faint tint if you wish, but avoid bright colours)

- layout kept simple (fancy logos, a variety of type fonts and varying type sizes reveal the beginner).

Correcting errors

Keep your manuscript neat and tidy. A single typing error will not exclude your manuscript from publication, but spell-checking and proofreading of the original manuscript is the freelance's work and it will annoy the editor if he has to do your job.

Of course you can use correction fluid and photocopies. Handwritten corrections, however, should be avoided. A single word can easily be misread by an editor or typesetter who is not familiar with your handwriting. If there are several typing errors in your manuscript, type it again.

Staple your pages firmly together, or, if the manuscript is too long to be stapled, number all pages and write the title next to each page number. Loose leaves get lost easily in the pile, and paper-clips tend to clip pages to the wrong manuscripts. It is not necessary to put your manuscript into a folder.

On top of your first page (or, if the feature runs over many pages, a cover sheet) write your name and address, the title, the type of manuscript (for example 'feature' or 'news article') and the word-count.

Counting the words

Please don't cheat with the word-count. You may write '1000 words' if your manuscript has 995 words or 1005. But don't claim to have a 1000 words feature if you have only 800 in the hope of getting better pay, or if the editor's word limit for features is 1200 and you did not know how to cut. False word-counts cause trouble during editorial production and editors don't take kindly to this.

Some editors like the word 'more' at the bottom of each page, and 'ends' at the bottom of the last one.

Don't worry if you cannot find a brilliant title for your feature. The editor is likely to change it anyway if it is not short or long enough to fit into the layout, or if it contains the same words as another heading in the same issue. However, you can help by writing several title suggestions in brackets under the initial title.

Intros and cross-heads

You can phrase the first paragraph so that it can be used as an 'intro', that is printed in a different typeface, catching the reader's eye. Freelances are not expected to write cross-heads (small subheadings). The graphic designers and layouters insert them if and where they look good and fill a gap.

If you want a word or sentence printed in italics, underline it in your manuscript. Don't use different typefaces and sizes, and avoid fancy logos and so on.

Always put the essential information at the beginning of your feature. A production editor who has to shorten a feature always cuts the last paragraph.

You can further help by attaching a contacts list to your manuscript, with names and telephone numbers of people and organisations mentioned, in case of urgent last-minute queries.

CHECKLIST

Before sending out the manuscript, ask yourself:

1.   Is this article of interest to the readers of the publication?

2.   Has a friend, tutor, or member of my writers' group read the article critically and suggested improvements?

3.   Have I proofread it carefully?

4.   Have I followed all the basic rules of presentation?

5.   Does the manuscript look neat and tidy?

6.   Does it contain my byline, my address and a word-count?

7.   Are the enclosures (photos with **captions**, sae) complete?

8.   Is the envelope strong enough for the manuscript?

9.   Is the postage sufficient?

10. Have I enclosed a letter suggesting further article ideas?

LOOKING AT EDITORIAL PRODUCTION

Lay people often believe that the editor accepts the manuscript and gives it to the printer. But the printer never sees the manuscript!

An accepted ms is either filed in the issue for which it has been commissioned, or held in stock for future use.

Often, editors cannot tell when they will be able to use a manuscript. How much editorial an issue contains depends on how much advertising space has been sold. The more successful the sale representatives have been, the more pages are allowed for editorial.

For technical reasons, magazine page numbers are normally multiples of eight or four. If an advertiser cancels a spread (a double page), the publisher has to cancel four pages, which means that two editorial pages have to be dropped. This may mean that your freelance feature has to be postponed to a later issue.

It can happen, however, that a one-page ad comes in at the last minute. Then the editor has to find material to fill three extra editorial pages. This is when he is glad to have good freelance material of varying length in stock. Perhaps an advertiser cancels his $1/4$-page ad, and the editor has to throw out a $1/4$-page feature and replace it by a $1/2$-page story.

When the editor says that he is going to use your story, but does not know when a slot will come up, he is telling the truth. Be patient.

The process varies greatly from one publishing house to another, but here is a typical example.

The subeditor marks up your manuscript, amending it to the house style, and sends it to the typesetters, who set and send the print outs (galleys) to the publisher's proofreader. The proofreader checks it for spelling mistakes which will be corrected by the typesetter. Increasingly, editors ask freelance journalists to submit copy on disk. This saves typesetting time. But check that your word processing software and disk format is acceptable for the publisher.

The production editor receives the corrected galleys. He selects the illustrations and instructs a layout artist on how to make up the pages, or makes them up himself. The galleys are cut and pasted on to cardboard templates, together with photocopies of the pictures, until everything fits. The page make-up can also be made on-screen (**desktop publishing**), usually by subeditors.

Often a word, a line or a paragraph has to be inserted to make the text fit into the allocated space. It looks odd if a column begins with the last line of a paragraph, so the production editor will pad out the text with a few extra words to fill the line.

The pasted pages, plus the floppy disk with the text (or the disk with the desktop published pages), are sent to the repro house who scan in the pictures and produce films of the pages. Print outs of the films (page proofs) are sent to the subeditor for approval, and then to the printers.

The printers produce a printing plate from the page film, then the publication is printed and later bound.

Your manuscript never gets further than the typesetters.

WHO IS THE EDITOR?

Readers, as well as writers, imagine that the editor, an all-important powerful person, gets involved in everything. This is rarely the case. Except with small press magazines, the editor-in-chief doesn't normally sort through the slush pile and send out rejection slips. He or she may not even decide about whom to commission to do what.

Much of the work which freelances think the editor does is done by other people on the editorial staff: the deputy editor, features editor, commissioning editor, desk editor, subeditor, production editor, editorial assistant and so on. Who is responsible for what differs from publication to publication. In this book the word 'editor' refers to the editorial team in general, not to the person of the editor-in-chief.

Letters addressed to 'The Editor' are usually opened by a secretary and distributed to the other editorial staff, in an attempt to keep as much away from the editor as possible.

The masthead or colophon, too, can be misleading. It may not list the full editorial staff, and the name of the person responsible for freelance manuscripts may be not included. Or the list may be padded out with fantasy names to impress readers, advertisers and competitors. In some one-person operations the editor puts down his name as well as three different pseudonyms and four job titles.

Sometimes, the editor-in-chief's name is added for prestige reasons only, and the person in question has little involvement with the publication. This may be the case when the magazine publishers like the prestige of using a reputable expert's name, and the expert of having the title 'editor'.

So to whom do you address your letters? 'Dear Editor' is acceptable initially if you don't know the name of the person. All further correspondence and queries should be addressed to whoever signed the response.

UNDERSTANDING EDITORS

It is often assumed that the editor is the most powerful person in the publishing house, that he decides what goes into the newspaper or magazine, thus influencing public opinion. This is not necessarily true.

Newspapers and magazines are financed mainly by advertising which provides about 80 per cent of the revenue, and according to the publisher's calculation, finance the editorial department including freelance fees. Subscriptions and over the counter sales pay for only 20 per cent — usually just enough to cover the distribution cost and postage. The advertising manager is often equal in rank to the editor.

Many advertisers are aware of their power and demand a nice editorial write up for their products, or threaten to cancel the annual advertising order if a friendly word about their competitors has been published.

Editors attempt to keep the editorial pages independent, despite the pressure from the advertising department. However, few publications can afford to ignore the advertisers' interests.

When I was deputy editor of a fashion magazine, we had the policy of 'two ed for one ad'. This meant that for every paid advertising page we had to publish two editorial pages promoting the advertiser. We fulfilled this condition by publishing photos of clothes from the advertiser's range, or perhaps an interview with their designer. In one case, the advertiser demanded that we published her sister-in-law's poems instead!

Sometimes we received a freelance manuscript along the lines How to Make Your Own Evening Gown. Our readers would have loved it — we had many readers' letters asking for information on the subject. But the main advertisers were producers of evening wear, and the DIY subject was taboo. Of course, we could not say so in the rejection slips.

What editors may not tell you

Many publishers try to turn the editorial department into a money-making organisation, not only by selling editorial space as 'advertising feature'. Some accept articles only if someone pays a contribution towards the production (usually called 'separation charges').

For example, your travel article about an exotic country may be perfect for a magazine and its readers, but if the relevant tourist board refuses to pay separation charges for colour photos, the editor may reject it in favour of a less exciting article about a country which offers to pay.

Travel, home furnishing, fashion and cosmetics are the areas where separation charges have become a habit for many publications.

Few editors are happy with this situation. Freelances should know that these commercial interests can be the reason behind a rejection.

HOW TO PLEASE AN EDITOR

Many freelances (particularly those whose ms have just been rejected) complain that editors are unfeeling, unfriendly, anonymous. But imagine yourself on the other side of the desk.

How editors see freelances

Some freelance writers are pleasant to work with. They are reliable people, full of initiative and ideas, who support editors with their knowledge and competence and save them much time.

Others appear to be impatient, unfriendly people, who demand time, work, patience and money and don't even bother to say thank you. They cheat with their invoices, get the facts in their features wrong and the editor into trouble — in short, they are a nuisance.

It may seem incredible, but there are more freelances of the second kind. Most editors come to the point where they refuse to even look at anything freelance-written. Friendly communications from freelances are rare.

Few writers thank the editor who has made the effort of explaining why he had to reject it. Hardly anyone bothers to say they are proud to write for the magazine, or how stunning the layout of their latest article looks in print.

Instead, editors get many letters accusing them of not reading manuscripts properly. An equal number complain about a changed phrase, a cut paragraph, or a boring layout. Add to that the freelances who blame the editor if the accepted feature does not appear in the next issue or if a cheque is delayed, and those who keep hinting that they find the magazine 'rather amateurish'. You get the picture.

Editors are not immune to flattery. Praise their publication, or their comment column. Say that you like the headline and the illustration which they have chosen to go with your story. Mention a feature they have published recently, which you have read with enthusiasm. Tell them that you are happy to have your feature accepted, and proud to write for their 'prestigious magazine' (the latter is particularly welcomed by editors of lesser-known publications).

Many freelances hesitate to write a friendly word to the editor, for fear that their efforts could be regarded as sycophantic. However, among so many letters of criticism a friendly word is always welcome.

When I was acting editor of a trade magazine, I put much time and work into editorial guidelines and sent them all to prospective contributors. One of them reacted immediately. 'Your guidelines are the best I have ever seen,' he wrote. 'Comprehensive and extremely helpful. I look forward to writing for you.' When his feature suggestions arrived, I recognised his name immediately.

Let the editor know — at once

Be reliable, and be honest. If the editor has expressed interest in your feature suggestion, and you have changed your mind and don't want to write it, let him know. If research takes up more time than expected and you feel that you can't make the **deadline**, contact the editorial department as soon as possible.

Write, rather than phone. Nothing annoys an editor more than phone calls when he is desperately trying to get pages ready for print. If you have to phone, don't ask for the editor personally. His deputy, the secretary, or the features editor can probably help you equally well. The best informed person in the department is usually the editorial assistant.

Secret files

Editors often approach each other for information about a journalist: 'This journalist wants to write a regular column for us. Is he reliable?' or 'I am looking for a contributor to cover the South East. Can you recommend someone?'

Each editor has a contributors' file. This can be a card system, or a computer data base. In addition to factual information, such as name, address, telephone, specialist subjects and rates, editors add comments.

Here is a selection of comments from the freelance file I've carried with me to whichever publication I was editing.

'Reliable, but always tries to get more pay.' 'Well researched features, but never keeps deadlines.' 'Pleasant person, keen to get a byline.' 'Writes too much, charges too much.' 'Good style, shows initiative.' 'Does not follow briefing, ms full of errors and handwritten corrections.' 'Initiative, brilliant ideas, well researched; style needs subbing.' 'Constantly threatens to stop submitting if we don't pay more, but always comes back.' 'Makes even legal subjects sound interesting.' 'Competent, reliable and highly professional.'

What notes have *your* editors written about *you*?

QUESTIONS AND ANSWERS

Q: Should I include the editors for whom I have written recently in my Christmas card list?

A: No. Sending a card would do no harm, but it is a waste of money. Every December the average editorial office is literally flooded with Christmas cards, most of them from public relations people. Chances that your card stands out and catches the editor's attention are small.

Q: How long should I wait for an editor's decision about a feature?

A: There are no hard and fast rules. The editorial staff on some publications work faster than on others. It also depends on the time of the year — in some months they are busier than in others. Give it a couple of months if it was an on spec submission or suggestion; three weeks if the editor has asked to see it; less if the article is a topical one.

Q: Can I ask the editor to explain the reason for rejecting my feature?

A: Yes, if the editor has asked to see the feature. He will probably give an explanation if you ask politely and don't challenge his decision. No, if it was an on spec submission. It is not an editor's job to teach you how to write better features.

KNOWING THE LAW

Copyright

There is no copyright on ideas or facts. If you read a feature about an interesting subject, and think you can write it better, then there is nothing to stop you from writing a feature based on this idea for another magazine.

Think twice, however, before you copy facts from other journalists' articles. You might be copying their mistakes. Always try to trace the original source.

The way someone puts words together to create a text is protected by copyright. If you like the introductory sentence of somebody's feature, you cannot just use it for your own article.

However, you are allowed to quote short extracts from other people's work, as long as you make it clear that it is a quote, and give the source. The law is not precise about how long these quotes can be. In practice, most journalists restrict their quotes to three sentences.

The Society of Authors has produced a guide on copyright which is available for £1.

Libel

Think twice before you embark on a campaign to ruin somebody's reputation. If this person brings a libel writ against you, you may be ruined financially. Libel laws are strict, and courts are likely to interpret them in the libelled person's favour. There is no affordable indemnity insurance which would protect freelance journalists.

However, you need not panic. If someone feels they have been libelled they can choose whether they take the bylined writer, or the editor, or the publisher to court. They usually choose the one from whom they can get most money. This is seldom the freelance scribe.

The laws are complex. Ask yourself: Is what I'm writing likely to damage someone's personal or professional reputation? If yes, be careful. The exception is, of course, the article which is clearly marked as a review.

If you think that a piece you are writing is potentially libellous, point it out to your editor, who can advise how to handle the situation, for example by phrasing a sentence carefully.

Invest £1 in the Society of Authors' guide to libel, or read the relevant section in the *Writers' and Artists' Yearbook.*

WHAT THE EDITORS SAY

I asked several editors what their pet hate is about freelances.

- Ian Boughton, group editor Trade Media Ltd (*Office Dealer, Office Secretary, Stationery Trade News, Greeting & Gift Stationer, Office Buyer*): 'Extending 400 words of meaningful content to make up the requested feature length of 1000 words is harder than it looks. Many freelances try to cheat, by padding the piece out with empty phrases. But the average freelance is not clever enough to get away with it. The experienced editor can spot padding a mile off. Padding is an insult to the person who commissioned the job. If I offer, say £150 for a 1000-word piece and feel compelled to cut out 400 words of unnecessary fluff, then I think I have a right to cut the fee accordingly.'

- Mary Bryce, deputy editor of *Chat:* 'Illiteracy.'

- Erika Harvey, editor of *Here's Health:* 'On spec contributors getting shirty if I don't get back to them quickly enough.'

- Hilary Robinson, features editor of *Good Housekeeping:* 'The ones who badger you for decisions the day after they sent the proposal.'

- Gail Robinson, editor of *What Personal Computer:* 'Not knowing the style of the magazine. Ringing to hassle.'

- Jane Simon, commissioning editor of *Woman:* 'Sloppiness. Getting facts wrong.'

- Martin Oxley, editor of *The Kent & Sussex Courier:* 'They don't carry mobile phones. We can't get in touch to ask them to cover an unexpected event.'

- John T Wilson, editor of *Great Ideas:* 'Poor presentation (for example, badly typed) and inadequate grasp of grammar.'

- Helene Hodge, managing editor of *Active Life:* 'People who ignore the specifications.'

And what makes the perfect contributor?

- Brian Attwood, editor of *The Stage and Television Today:* 'News sense, brevity, topicality.'

- Gail Robinson, editor of *What Personal Computer:* 'Flexibility, reliability, meets deadlines, checks all details.'

- Suzanne Riley, editor of *Quartos:* 'Knowing where the manuscript is going before writing it.'

- Diana K Jones, editor of *The Disabled Driver:* 'Style, impact, presentation, content, newsability.'

- Mary Bryce, deputy editor of *Chat:* 'Understands brief, delivers on deadline (preferably earlier), punchy writing style.'

- Martin Oxley, editor of *The Kent & Sussex Courier:* 'Determination and writing style are taken for granted. Going to the right person or the right paper at the right time makes the difference.'

- Helene Hodge, editor of *Active Life:* 'Knowing the market, good research, writing skills; delivering to brief and on time.'

- John T Wilson, editor of *Great Ideas:* 'Someone who can understand a journal's needs and meet those needs by good research, competent writing and empathy with the readers.'

- Erika Harvey, editor of *Here's Health:* 'Willing to do research. Takes note of magazine style. Follows commission brief. Checks facts.'

- Steve Windsor, managing editor of *Practical Fishkeeping:* 'Knowing the potential readership. Hitting deadlines.'

- Jane Simon, commissioning editor of *Woman:* 'Understanding the publication.'

- Michael Furnell, editor of *Stamp Lover:* 'A wide knowledge of life in general and a specialisation in one or two important subjects.'

- Peter Merring, editor of *Steam Classic:* 'Aside from the fundamental skills — such as literacy — the ability to follow a brief, to present the material in an acceptable fashion and to absorb and follow the grammatical/typographical style of a publication.'

- Charlotte Collis, editor of *Popular Crafts Magazine:* 'A good freelance can adapt easily to the style of a certain title, gets work in on time and well presented, and is not put off by the first rejection.'

10
Illustrating Your Articles

BUYING A CAMERA

Choose a camera which is lightweight, and quick and easy to handle. Autofocus cameras are ideal for freelance journalists. Choose one which has a zoom, enabling you to take pictures from a 'non-threatening' distance, which means that people behave more naturally when you photograph them. It is also easier to get around unwanted lamp posts and cars in the foreground.

Go for the best lens you can afford. Make sure the camera has a lens cap, if possible built in. Scratched lenses and lost caps are frequent problems.

Some camera shops sell good second-hand cameras with a six-month guarantee.

For most publications, including glossy magazines, pictures taken with small autofocus cameras are acceptable and reproduce well, provided they are sharp in focus.

A higher level of technical perfection is essential to get photos accepted for full-page size publication or for cover pages.

THE SUBJECT COUNTS

Try to take several photos of every subject you write about. Editors like photos which show people in general, children, good-looking young women and men, animals and action, and depict atmosphere.

A CRASH COURSE IN PRESS PHOTOGRAPHY

If you write about a business woman or a craftsman, show her or him at work — at the desk or the telefax, with the hammer or chisel. The article is illustrated much better with an 'action' picture rather than a shot where the person sits or stands stiffly, not knowing what to do with their hands.

When taking photos of a theatre play or dress rehearsal, show a colourful, dynamic scene with two or three people, rather than a stiff group shot.

Avoid pictures of mayors. They have several appointments per day and the readers of the local newspapers get bored with the same face on every page. Equally boring is the picture of two people standing parallel to each other while shaking hands — this is an unnatural pose. Avoid cheque presentations to charities; take a photo of the activity which raised the money instead.

When taking a shot of a general scene — say, a fun fair, a folk dance festival or a crowded beach on a hot summer's day — make sure you get people's faces rather than their backs. Focus on a small child. Take a picture which makes readers think 'how cute'. Alternatively, you can focus on a pretty young girl or a handsome bloke. They should come across as friendly and cheerful, with subtle sex appeal.

Travel editors are not interested in photos of landscapes and famous buildings, which are available free from tourist boards. Shots of native crafts people at work are bestsellers, followed by pictures of handsome men and women, cute children, and animals in their natural habitat.

Bright red is every picture editor's favourite colour. So watch out for red dresses in the crowd, red fruit at the market stalls, red shorts at the sports festival, red balloons in the sky.

COLOUR OR BLACK-AND-WHITE?

Some publications use only colour (referred to as '4c'), some only black-and-white (b/w) photography. Is it possible for the editor to have colour pictures reproduced in black-and-white? It is. However, the result is not always satisfactory, and never as good as if the photo had been taken in black-and-white. Reasonable results can be achieved if the photo has strong light-dark contrasts and clear lines.

The printing procedure often requires that some pages are printed in 4c, others in b/w, which have to be in a specific order. Publishing a single 4c photo on a b/w page can mean, for example, that eight full pages have to be printed in 4c. This can cost a fortune, so don't be disappointed if your photo appears in b/w print although other parts of the magazine have been published in colour. Editors often have to decide at short notice which features to publish on 4c or b/w pages.

When to choose transparencies

The reproduction quality from a slide or transparency ('tranny') is always better than from a print, particularly if the picture is to appear in a large format. However, trannies are expensive, and if you don't want to send your originals you may have to spend a considerable amount to have them duplicated. Colour prints are acceptable for most publications, unless they are intended for a full page or the cover. Travel magazines often insist on trannies.

Unfortunately, it is not possible to have transparencies made from print film. If you have used print film only while you were in Sri Lanka, and the editor insists on trannies, there is nothing you can do. You could have your print photos photographed onto slide film, but the resulting quality won't satisfy an editor.

Some photographers send colour prints, noting on the reverse 'Tranny available on request'. This is a sensible and perfectly acceptable solution, except for urgent commissioned work.

Does size matter?

Size is unimportant. Large prints give better reproduction quality, but are damaged more easily than small prints. Postcard size is usually a convenient solution.

The situation is more difficult with trannies: 50 per cent of all editors prefer the small, mounted format (which they can use in a projector), the other 50 per cent say that the larger size is more convenient on a lightbox.

TO CROP OR NOT TO CROP?

Many books and features on photography have one weakness in common: they are written by freelance photographers, not editors, and fail to present editorial requirements from the editor's point of view.

If you are serious about submitting your photos for publication, forget anything you have ever read about cropping, for example. Tight cropping, that is cutting away as much background as possible to create an unusual composition or to focus on the main motif, may earn you a prize in photographic competitions. But it will also, almost certainly, earn you a rejection slip from the editor.

Editors prefer as much background as possible, the more boring, the better. 'Unnecessary' background allows, for example, for cropping a 'landscape' (horizontal) format into a 'portrait' (vertical), a square or any other shape required by the layout, without cutting away any essential material. Editors frequently have to reject photos because they would need three more millimetres on either side — possibly the three millimetres the freelance has previously cropped to create a special effect.

A professional production editor has much more experience at cropping than you have, and will bring out your photos to their best advantage. Of course you can, alternatively, submit one portrait and one landscape version of each photo, but photos with a lot of background still stand a better chance of publication.

If you ignore the advice given in books on photography, and *don't* cut away that large chuck of boring, pale grey sky, the editor has the opportunity to print the headline, the introductory paragraph, or a caption into it, a layout style which is particularly popular with magazines. Of course, your main motif must be clear in focus and cover most of the picture. There's no use in sending a photo where the main subject accounts for only a tenth of the picture.

CAPTIONING

If you can think of a witty caption, fine, but more importantly it must be informative. The editor will use the information supplied to write a caption which fits into the available space.

It is your job, not the editor's, to find out the names, titles and positions of all the people in the photo. Ask them as soon as you've taken the picture; it will be difficult to get the relevant information afterwards. Keep pen and notebook at hand. The caption must also contain the venue, the event, and the date when the picture was taken.

SUBMITTING PHOTOS

Take care to label your photos correctly with photographer's name and address, subject pictured, title or caption suggestion, date when taken, full names and titles of all people in the photo, if and for how long the photo may be held in stock. Self-adhesive labels are better than ballpoint pens, which can damage the picture, and felt-tip pens or rubber stamps which tend to smear. Typed labels are preferred to handwritten notes. When submitting trannies, give the basic information on the mount or bag and number them (*eg* 'Smith — council meeting — 4') and attach a list with detailed information.

Take care with the packaging, use strong envelopes. You can buy cardboard-lined or padded envelopes, but it is cheaper to use ordinary ones and cut your cornflakes boxes into A5 size. A self-addressed, stamped envelope should be enclosed. As this can be difficult and expensive, you may use stamped, self-addressed 're-use envelope' labels instead. The editor can re-use the padded envelope in which you have sent the pics.

Ninety-nine per cent of all glass-mounted trannies arrive with broken glass, however well padded the envelope is. Cardboard mounts are safer and cheaper. And if you submit a series of trannies, the editors appreciate them in clear plastic presentation bags available in photo shops.

HOW TO GET YOUR PICTURES BACK

Many photos and trannies get lost in the production process, either in the editorial office, at the lithographer's or the printer's. Always keep your negatives. You can have duplicates made from transparencies; this costs about £1.20 each. The dupes are usually very good, although the colours may not be quite as strong.

If you require your photos back after publication, write 'please return to. . .' on each of them. However, it can take weeks until the editors receive them from the repro house, and even longer until they find the time to return them to you.

WHAT THE EDITORS SAY

Editors' requirements differ.

● Diana K Jones, editor of *The Disabled Driver:* 'I welcome illustrations. They must be crystal clear for good reproduction, and accurately highlight the feature content. They must be interesting and give impact.'

● Ian Boughton, editor of *Stationery Trade News:* 'It is surprising how many freelance pieces are submitted with no thought to illustration at all. When I have raised the point, the nearest I've ever got to a creative answer is the suggestion that I approach a picture library (have you seen their prices?!) or that I ring up the manufacturers in that sector and ask them to send a selection. Why doesn't the freelance ring them?

'If a story needs pictures to make a complete story, then pictures with text make a complete freelance job. Don't say that your job is the words, not the pics. You won't get away with it. Think about illustrations before the editor asks.'

- Kathryn Joyce, editorial secretary of *PC Magazine:* 'We don't require illustrations — we have an in-house photographer.' *Here's Health* and *Great Ideas* don't require pictures either.

- Martin Oxley, editor of *The Kent & Sussex Courier:* 'We want photos only if they are good, preferably colour prints.'

- Mary Bryce, deputy editor of *Chat*, Gail Robins, editor of *What Personal Computer*, and Helene Hodge, editor of *Active Live*, all say: 'Illustrations — slides if possible *are very important.'*

- Hilary Robinson, features editor of *Good Housekeeping*, also asks for slides. 'If the contributor cannot supply pictures, then at least the interviewees must be willing to be photographed.'

- Charlotte Collis, editor of *Popular Crafts Magazine:* 'Photographs for publication should ideally be on medium format transparency. Discuss the style in advance.'

- Michael Furnall, editor of *Stamp Lover:* 'I welcome photos, black-and-white for preference.'

- Steve Windsor, managing editor of *Practical Fishkeeping* and *Fishkeeping Answers*, and Jane Simon, commissioning editor of *Woman*, both say: 'Colour photos — slides or prints — are essential.'

- Brian Attwood, editor of *The Stage and Television:* 'We welcome photos as long as they are offered free. We can't afford a hefty freelance bill.'

- Peter Merring, editor of *Steam Classic:* 'We are always looking for good, interesting illustrations. Basic advice: check the picture is sharp and don't send under- or over-exposed pics.'

11
Managing Money Matters

NEGOTIATING YOUR FEE

Freelance journalism is a buyer's market. Supply exceeds demand by far, and the buyers, the editors, dictate prices. As a freelance you have the choice to sell either at market price, or not at all. Rates vary greatly, with small press and women's magazines at the bottom and business and technical publications at the top end of the scale.

If bylines are more important to you than profit, or if a publication has standard rates, simply add to your query letter the phrase 'at your usual rates'.

Editors who say that payment is made 'by arrangement' expect an indication of your price range. The sentence 'My usual rates are between £60 and £120' shows that you are a professional.

The editor understands that for £60 you will supply a good feature, and for £120 probably an even better one. She also knows that if she can offer only £50, a compromise is possible, but if her maximum is £10 it is not worth wasting her time and yours.

Avoiding disappointment

Freelances and editors have one thing in common: a strong dislike for discussing the financial side. Freelances are afraid to appear greedy, while editors are embarrassed that they cannot afford to pay NUJ (National Union of Journalists) rates. But if payment is not discussed in advance, disappointment is inevitable.

Once I was present at the discussion between an editor and a prospective contributor. Every aspect of editorial requirements was discussed in detail, and only after two hours did it become clear that the freelance expected a minimum rate of £200, and the editor, with the best will in the world, could not afford more than £20.

Editors are grateful if you open the financial discussion frankly and at an early stage, to save time and embarrassment for both of you.

Most editors are aware of how much time and effort goes into freelance journalism and would like to pay good rates. However, their position is that of business managers, employed to buy the best possible material at the lowest possible price. The budgets are often very tight. If they buy your feature, they have to reject another one. If they agree to pay you a higher rate, they have to cut back on somebody else's.

Often, they are deeply ashamed that they cannot pay a freelance as much as his work is worth. Many freelances add to the embarrassment by assuming an arrogant smile and a contemptuous voice when talking about money matters, and this does not help.

If you are unsure how much to ask, begin the negotiation by stating your normal rates, perhaps with a wide 'between . . . and . . .' rate.

Maybe the editor will take the first step and quote a figure. If you think you could get more it is fair to say 'I had hoped for £120'. Freelances usually succeed if they ask for 20 per cent more than offered (if they have approached the editor with a feature), or even 50 per cent more (if the editor has approached them).

GETTING AN INCREASE

As a regular contributor whose services have been valued over a considerable period, you'll probably be looking for a rise. This is a reasonable request, but the subject must be approached diplomatically.

If you tell the editor that you need the money because you have to feed a family and pay a high mortgage, she may feel for you, but is unlikely to give you an increase. Blackmail does not pay either.

When I was working for *European Frozen Food Buyer* and *European Drinks Buyer*, we paid £80/1000 words. Not a fortune, but not bad either. Some contributors wrote unpleasant letters threatening that unless we tripled the rates immediately they would stop submitting. They were quickly replaced. All of them, without exception, came back after a while, saying that they had not meant it so seriously and of course they would be happy to write at the usual rate . . . too late.

The one and only reason which will convince the editor to give you a rise is that you can give her a better product to justify the higher price. Explain what you could do even better than before if paid more, and how the publication would benefit from it: for example more detailed research, foreign contacts, manuscript submissions on disk, etc.

Invoice

Invoice number: 0015

Date: 28 November 199x

Payable by: 31 December 199x

From:
Nigel Nickeling
1, Abcde Lane
Fghijkl Town YY1 1ZZ
Tel (0000) 00000

To:
You and Your House
Att. Doreen Dorian, Editor

Publication date	Item	Words/ Quantity	Rate	Amount
15 November 199x	Feature 'How to make your home burglarproof'	800	62.50/1000	£ 50.00
	Photo 'Installing window locks'	1	20	£ 20.00
22 November 199x	Feature 'How to save money on heating bills'	1000	62.50/1000	£ 62.50
	Photos for illustration	3	20	£ 60.00
				————
				£192.60

Fig. 16. Invoice.

GETTING PAID

Some publications pay on acceptance, but most on publication. Checking every issue, week after week, to see if your article is printed can be nerve-wracking! Always ask the editor to send you a free copy of the issue which contains your work.

While some publishers send a cheque automatically as soon as the article is printed, others require an invoice. It is a good idea to send out invoices anyway, because they create a professional impression. If you have registered your journalism business for VAT, you must send invoices in any case.

Invoices can be done on your computer or typewriter. You can also buy a duplicate invoice book, fill in the invoice forms by hand, send the original to the editor and keep the duplicate in the book. This is the quickest and most practical way.

Address your invoices to the person who has accepted the feature. It should contain the word 'invoice', your name and address, the invoice date and invoice number, the title of the feature, the dates of acceptance and publication, the length, the agreed rate, the overall price, and if applicable, VAT. You may add 'payable by' (insert a date four weeks after publication) to speed up payment.

MAKING PUBLISHERS PAY SOONER

Don't cover several features with one invoice. Accountants are in the habit of paying small invoices quickly, and putting large invoices aside until some money comes in. If the company has a cash flow problem, they may spread payment of your ten invoices at £100 each over three months, but if you send one invoice for £1000 you may have to wait a year!

A number of accountants unfortunately tend to think of writers as artists who should not demand payment, and therefore regard writers' invoices as 'unimportant'. Send a business-like reminder, addressed to the accounts department, where your invoice and the chequebook usually are. It is not the editor's job, at least not in major publishing houses, to chase up overdue payments for you. The reminder should be polite, matter-of-fact, and repeat all the information contained in the invoice.

Four weeks' delay justifies a first reminder, eight weeks a second. After that, it is time for a phone call. Most freelances make the mistake of being very rude, and consequently unsuccessful. Learn from profes-

Reminder

Date: 15 January 199x

Invoice number:	0015
Date of invoice	28 November 199x
Payable by:	31 December 199x

From:
Nigel Nickeling
1, Abcde Lane
Fghijkl Town YY1 1ZZ
Tel (0000) 00000

To:
You and Your House
Att. Doreen Dorian, Editor

May I remind you that payment for the following items is now overdue:

Publication date	Item	Words/ Quantity	Rate	Amount
15 November 199x	Feature 'How to make your home burglarproof'	800	62.50/1000	£ 50.00
	Photo 'Installing window locks'	1	20	£ 20.00
22 November 199x	Feature 'How to save money on heating bills'	1000	62.50/1000	£ 62.50
	Photos for illustration	3	20	£ 60.00
				————
				£192.60

Fig. 17. Reminder.

sional credit control people, who enquire in a pleasant tone: 'Good afternoon, I wonder if you can help me. My name is Cathy Clever, and my invoice dated 10 October is still outstanding. I wonder if there is a problem?'

Note that this is an enquiry, not an accusation. The accountant who remembers your friendly voice will find it more difficult to ignore your invoice. The phone call gives the company a chance to sort out a compromise. For example, if cash flow is their problem you may agree on payment by instalments.

If this doesn't help, write a final polite letter, say that unless you are paid in full within two weeks you will take the matter to the small claims court. Professional journalists say that this method always works — probably because accountants take legal matters seriously.

Still unsuccessful? Most likely the publishing house is in serious financial difficulties. Take your case to the small claims court before it is too late.

If you experience regular problems in getting your money from a publishing house, stop writing for them.

12
Going Freelance

ARE YOU READY TO TAKE THE PLUNGE?

Becoming a full-time freelance journalist means starting your own business. This needs careful thought and preparation. Don't give up your full-time job until you have mastered the craft and established good contacts with editors. Most journalists slipped gradually into self-employment, writing articles in their spare time, while earning a regular income from a staff job.

It pays to enrol on a course on how to start your own business, as well as a course on marketing skills, or personal selling skills. A good book to read is *How to Start a Business From Home* by Graham Jones. You can also get free booklets from banks.

Ask yourself the following questions:

- Am I a good journalist? Have I mastered the craft? Do I have a portfolio of published work?

- Do I have the contacts and the markets? Do editors recognise my name as an expert in my field? Are they willing to buy more of my work?

- Do I have enough ideas for articles?

- Has my average income from writing in the last six months been at least £50 per 1000 words?

- Has 50 per cent or more of the work I have written in the last 12 months been accepted for publication?

- Am I willing to take the risk? Can I cope with irregular income? Do I have any dependants? Do I have financial reserves to live on until the money for published articles comes in?

- Do I possess the necessary marketing skills, and the assertiveness to sell myself and my work?

- Do I have the self-discipline to work 40 hours a week (or whatever target I have set myself), shutting out distractions such as neighbours calling, the pile of ironing in the corner and the tempting novel on the bedside table?

- Can I keep going when times are tough, when there is a period of nothing but rejection slips?

RAISING THE FINANCE

Setting yourself up as a journalist needs little money. But you must have enough to pay for day-to-day expenses such as the phone bill and postage stamps, and a reserve to live on until money comes in.

One of the hazards of being a freelance journalist is that you don't get paid when you submit your work, but when it has been published. Many months may pass between acceptance and publication.

You may be eligible for financial help. The Enterprise Allowance Scheme offers free business training and weekly payments between £20 and £60 for a year if you have been out of work for at least six weeks. You must commit yourself to work at least 30 hours per week, to open a business bank account, keep detailed books and meet your adviser once every three months. You are not allowed to do freelance work before your business plan is approved, but you can do market research. 'Writers' are often not accepted (probably because the organisers imagine a writer will spend £2000 on an exotic holiday and return with the inspiration for a single headline), but 'journalists' are. Details differ from county to county. Contact your nearest Enterprise Agency.

Arts councils also give grants, usually towards a training course. You must prove that you earn most of your income from freelance work, and in this case it is better to describe your occupation as 'writer' than as 'journalist'.

There are many other grants, scholarships, sponsorships and awards available. Ask everyone who might know about something: the Enterprise agency, the chamber of commerce, the town and borough councils, writers' groups, journalism organisations, arts councils. But ask before you start your business.

PRESENTING A BUSINESS PLAN

A business plan shows you — and any potential sponsor — how likely your enterprise is to succeed. Answer the following questions in detail to develop a basic plan.

1. What experience, knowledge, training or experience do you have? For example, your work experience at a magazine's editorial office, and your experience in writing freelance in your spare time.

2. What are your personal strengths (for example, determination, selling skills) and weaknesses (for example, shyness)?

3. Describe your product (articles and features), your customers (publications) and the consumers (readers). What benefits do the publications and the readers get from your articles?

4. What is your survival income? How much do you need to cover your personal expenditure?

5. What do you want to achieve, and when? For example, to sell 20 features in two months.

6. How often will editors buy your features? How many will be regular customers, and how many will be one-offs?

7. Who are your competitors (other journalists who write about the same subject)? What are their strengths and weaknesses, and how much do they earn per 1000 words?

8. How long does it take you to write a 1000-word feature? How long to research it? How much do you want to, or have to, earn per 1000 words?

9. Describe how you do market research. For example, studying magazines and newspapers.

10. Describe your marketing strategy. For example, writing query letters.

11. How much money will you invest in equipment?

12. How much profit (income minus expenses) do you have to make to break even?

13. How much time will you spend on marketing, and how much on administration (for example, keeping books, filing)?

14. How many features can you sell per month, realistically? How much money can you earn per month?

15. How many days, weeks or months are likely to pass before you receive the money you have earned?

16. Make a profit or loss forecast. This is a table which shows how much money you spend and earn each month. The difference between the two is your profit or loss. During the first few months you may make a loss, because you are investing in equipment. But after a few months you must make a profit, otherwise your business is not viable.

17. Make a cash flow forecast. This shows the money coming into, and going out of, your bank account and purse.

    For example, the editor accepts a feature and promises to pay £200. You have earned £200, and enter it in the profit and loss. Two months later, you receive the cheque. Now you enter £200 in the cash flow.

    Preparing cash flow and profit and loss forecasts takes time. It is easiest with pre-printed forms which you can get free from most banks.

PAYING TAX AND VAT

As soon as you open your business, you must notify the Inland Revenue. You are due to pay income tax at the end of the business year. How much you pay depends on your income, expenses and profits. You must keep detailed books.

You also must register with the Contributions Agency and pay National Insurance contributions. If you are a full-time freelance journalist you register for Class 2.

You don't have to pay VAT unless your turnover exceeds a certain amount which you as a freelance journalist are unlikely to achieve. However, you may choose to register voluntarily. This means extra paperwork, but it allows you to claim back VAT on items you bought for your business. For example, if you bought an expensive computer, and don't expect to earn a lot during the first year of business, you may get a considerable VAT refund.

Details change frequently, but you can get free booklets which explain the ins and outs of VAT, income tax and National Insurance contributions in plain English (see Further Reading).

The applicant is required to give particulars of her journalistic, literary or allied work:

STAFF MEMBERS:
Please give name of magazine or newspaper.

....

Position on staff ....

BOOKS, POETRY, PLAYS:
Titles, publishers and dates of publication &/or production

STORIES, ARTICLES ETC.:
Periodicals in which contributions have appeared and dates of publication.

TELEVISION, FILM, VIDEO and RADIO SCRIPTS:
Brief particulars.

ALLIED WORK:
Including research, photography, illustrating, etc. Brief particulars as above.

Please attach brief additional information if necessary, together with s.a.e. for reply.

THE SOCIETY OF WOMEN WRITERS AND JOURNALISTS

President: Nina Bawden, F.R.S.L.

APPLICATION FOR FULL MEMBERSHIP

Completed application form should be sent to:
Hon Membership secretary:— Christine Fagg,
33 Priory Way, Hitchin, Herts, SG4 9BL

Fig. 18. Application form for full SWWJ membership.

APPLICATION FOR FULL MEMBERSHIP

Applications can normally only be considered if sponsored by two persons who are either (a) Full Members of the society, or (b) Editors or Publishers, or (c) Persons of equivalent standing, e.g. Radio or T.V. Producers, etc. who have personal knowledge of the Applicant's published work.

(Associate Members should complete the relevant portions of this form)

(Please TYPE or use BLOCK CAPITALS)
Name in full (stating Title, Mrs. Miss, Ms etc.)

....

Name(s) under which you write. ....

....

Nationality or Country ....

Any occupation other than writing ....

Address ....

....

Telephone. ....

Signature ....

Date ....

SPONSORS.

(Sponsors, Proposer and Seconder should sign the declaration below. If no sponsors available please state reason)

Proposer's Declaration:

I wish to sponsor the application of

....
(Name of Applicant)

for membership of the society. I have personal knowledge of her work and consider her to be a writer of professional ability and experience.

Proposer's Name (in capitals)..

Signed..

Status of Proposer
(SWWJ full member, Editor, Publisher, or person of equivalent standing)
Address ....

....

Telephone No. ....

Seconder's Name (in capitals)..

Signed ....

Status of Seconder
(as for proposer)

Address ....

....

Telephone No. ....

Election of a member shall be determined by a majority vote of the Council

131

APPLICATION FOR PROBATIONARY MEMBERSHIP

The applicant is required to give full particulars opposite of any work which she has had published.

A published applicant *without* sponsors is required in addition to submit photocopies of a minimum of 4 pieces of her published work.

An unpublished writer (with or without sponsors) or a published writer with less than 4 pieces of work to her credit, is required to submit up to 3 mss. together totalling not more than 6,000 words. (This may be work-in-progress e.g. a chapter of a book, articles, poems, stories or a scene from a play, or work specially written for this application.)

Submissions must be accompanied by 3 envelopes, large enough to take the mss. (2 envelopes stamped but *not* addressed and 1 stamped and self-addressed). These are required in order that the mss. can be sent to a professional reader for assessment and then presented to the Council of the SWWJ with the application for membership. Care will be taken of the submissions and they will in due course be returned but the Society cannot accept responsibility for their safety. PLEASE MAKE SURE THAT YOU RETAIN COPIES OF YOUR SUBMISSIONS.

If accepted, membership will be subject to re-consideration at the end of TWO YEARS, during which time the Probationary Member is expected to work towards the attainment of a full professional standard, thereby becoming eligible for FULL membership of the Society.

(Please write in BLOCK CAPITALS)
Full Name (stating Mrs. Miss. Ms. etc.)......................

Pseudonyms used (if any)......................

Nationality......................
Address...................... Postcode..........

Telephone Number......................

If possible please give names of 2 sponsors, who should be either FULL members of the SWWJ or editors, publishers or persons of equivalent literary standing.

Name of sponsor......................
Status......................
Name of sponsor......................
Status......................

PARTICULARS OF PUBLISHED WORK (if any)
giving dates, names and publisher(s) and titles of mss.

Fig. 19. Application form for probationary SWWJ membership.

JOINING A PROFESSIONAL ORGANISATION

When you become a member of a journalists' or writers' organisation you get advice, support (usually moral, but in some cases legal too), information, motivation and contacts.

Most organisations demand that you are a semi-professional, or professional, writer. Some, like the Society of Authors or International PEN, accept only writers who have had at least one book published for full membership. Others are open only to women (for example, the Society of Women Writers and Journalists or the Women Writers Network), or to journalists who specialise in a subject (for example, the British Guild of Travel Writers).

Members are entitled to print 'member of. . .' in their letterheads, which shows that you are a professional.

Writers who are not yet professionals may not join, although they can attend many events and seminars for a small fee.

The Society of Women Writers and Journalists offers 'probationary membership' for aspiring writers who have had only a few pieces published. Probationary members have the same benefits as full members (except they may not use it on their letterheads), and after two years they are expected to achieve semi-professional level and become full members. (For details of organisations see Useful Addresses.)

SELECTING THE TOOLS OF THE TRADE

Equipping your office for little money

You don't need a lot to set yourself up as a freelance journalist. Here is a selection of useful items. Only you can decide what you need immediately, and which purchases you want to postpone until later.

Stationery
- A lot of white A4 paper. Buy it in bulk from your local printer.

- Envelopes in varying sizes. You can get them much cheaper if you buy them in boxes of a thousand. Consider sharing a pack with other writers.

- Postage stamps. Except for topical news items, you can send out your queries and features second class and save money.

- A clippings book to keep your published articles in.

- Lots of suspension files, to file your published articles, sample features and research notes. Suspension files are cheapest if bought in packs of 50 or more.

- Box files, ringbinders and magazine files. Wait until your stationery supplier has them on special offer.

- Printed letterheads, with your name, address, and the membership of journalists' and writers' organisations. Shop around. Prices differ from printer to printer. By negotiating you often get a better deal. Five hundred letterheads, printed in one colour on good tinted paper, cost about £60 plus VAT. The more you order, the lower the price per sheet. The printer may charge you extra for the design.

- Compliment slips, similar in design and contents to the letterheads. Three hundred compliment slips cost around £25 plus VAT.

- Business cards. Instead of ordering them from your printer, use one of the instant print machines which you can find at many post offices and railway stations. At the printer's you would pay around £45 plus VAT for 200 cards. At the machine you get them for £3 per 50, including VAT.

Office equipment
- A typewriter. You can buy a good one second-hand at a car boot sale for under £15. Try it out, and make sure it is a brand for which ribbons are still available.

- A telephone. Ask British Telecom for an itemised bill if you are using your private phone for business purposes. If you decide to have a separate extension for your business, BT will charge you for the installation.

- A telephone answering machine, so that editors can leave a message at any time. You can buy one second-hand.

- A telefax machine. It's often cheaper to send a fax than to make a phone call, which helps keep down research costs, and faxes are great for urgent manuscripts. Telefax paper is cheapest if you buy at least five rolls at a time.

- Instead of a telefax, a telephone and a telephone answering machine, you can buy a machine which combines all three. Choose one which also allows you to take copies. These are not as good as proper photocopies, but the facility is useful when you're in a hurry. It should also have a facility to record your telephone conversations (for example, for telephone interviews). It is important that the machine recognises if an incoming call is a fax or a phone message, and switches automatically to either the fax or the answerphone when you're not there. Don't buy a combined machine second-hand: you have to switch manually from fax to answerphone and back, which is useless if an editor wants to send you a fax and you're not there.

- A word processor or computer, plus software and printer. (See below.)

Furniture

- A writing desk, perhaps with a return unit for your typewriter or computer. You can buy a good one from a dealer in used office furniture for around £50.

- A comfortable office chair, with adjustable height and back. You will spend a lot of time sitting at your desk. A second-hand office chair costs around £35.

- A mobile drawer unit for extra storage space, and on which you can place your printer or telefax (about £25 second-hand).

- A filing cabinet for suspension files (between £30 and £60 for a second-hand one with four drawers, depending on its condition).

THE WRITER IN THE COMPUTER AGE

Word processing is increasingly important in journalism. This section introduces you to the basics you need to know about the subject. It helps you to decide if you want to buy a computer, and if so, which. But it cannot make the decision for you. Remember that computers and programmes are updated frequently and prices change quickly. Regard this section as the starting point from which to start your own investigation.

Do I need a computer?

You can be a successful writer without ever touching a computer. On the other hand, it is easier and quicker to make changes to a manuscript if you have it on your computer. For example, you can insert or delete whole sections, or move paragraphs around, without retyping the page.

With a computer you can produce more work during your working hours. This can help increase your income. On the other hand, computers are an expensive investment, and you have to write many features to recoup the money.

If the only reason why you are not earning a fortune is that you spend too much time retyping your manuscripts, then a computer is a worthwhile investment. But if you don't earn a fortune because all your manuscripts come back with rejection slips, then a computer won't help.

True, you can produce ten times as much work with a computer. If you normally write and sell two articles per week, you can write and sell 20 with a computer. But if you write two articles per week and they don't normally get published, then you will probably produce 20 articles per week which still won't get published.

Do editors require word processed copy?

More and more editors welcome manuscript submissions on disks, which save typesetting costs. Some editors ask contributors if they have a modem to mail copy electronically. The use of modern technology in the communication between writers and editors is increasing. However, no magazine or newspaper editor will reject a good feature which arrives on his desk in traditional format.

What do I need?

Even if you don't know anything about computers, you know — better than any computer dealer — what you are going to use it for, now or in future. Once you've made up your mind what you want to do, every good dealer can advise you on the best computer. Ask yourself:

- Am I the only person who will be using the computer? Are my spouse/children/employees going to use it?

- How many hours per day will I be using it?

- In addition to writing articles, what else will I do on the computer? Book-keeping? Desktop publishing? Games? Write a novel? Edit a newsletter?

- Do I want to exchange data (manuscripts) with editors? If so, what equipment do these editors use?

- Am I familiar with using computers? What experience do I have? How confident am I about learning new software?

- If I have never used a computer before, how confident am I?

- If I need tuition, where can I get it and how much is it going to cost?

- What is the maximum I can afford to pay?

Once you are clear in your mind, you can start shopping around. The items you need are a computer, a printer, a screen, a keyboard and word processing software. Often, you get a good deal if you buy a package which contains some or all of these items. However, the printer is seldom included in package deals and it is one of the most expensive items.

Make sure that the screen is a non-glare, low radiation one. You will be spending a lot of time at the computer. The keyboard should be a special hardwearing model — even the busiest secretary doesn't type as much non-stop as a writer does.

Where do I buy a computer?

Just pop in to some computer stores, explain what you want and ask questions. Chain stores tend to offer lower prices, but less expertise and after-sales service. The same applies to computers bought by mail order.

When comparing prices, ask what period of warranty is included. If you have to pay extra for extended warranty it makes the purchase more expensive.

Choose a supplier whom you trust, and avoid those who talk to you in an arrogant or patronising tone. Ask other writers where they bought their computers, and how pleased they are with their purchases and the after-sales service.

What computer do I need?

This depends on what you want to do with it. Many journalists are happy with PCWs (from Amstrad). Their main advantage is that they are more affordable than personal computers or Applemacs. The disadvantage is that their disk format is not compatible with other computers, so you cannot exchange disks with an editor.

Applemacs (from Mackintosh) are considered to work fast and to be especially strong on graphics and design. This is why many publishers, especially newspapers, use them in their editorial departments. It seems that the newspapers publishers' preferred software packages for Applemacs are WordPerfect (for word processing) and Quark XPress (for desktop publishing). Applemacs are relatively expensive. Their disks can be used only on other Applemacs, not on personal computers.

Personal computers (PCs) are probably the most versatile option.

Most of them are compatible, which means they can use the same software and disk formats. Prices depend on the brand name, the memory and many other factors. For journalism, you don't need much memory capacity, but if you are thinking of doing desktop publishing it is better to buy a computer with sufficient memory.

Choose a PC which has a hard disk drive (on which you do your work) as well as a 3.5'' disk drive (so that you can take file and backup copies, and send disks to editors). You don't need an extra CD ROM drive for journalistic work.

How do I choose my software?

The only software you need for journalism is one for word processing. You must buy a version which has been designed for your particular computer. A basic word processing software program which costs around £40 is sufficient for writing and editing articles. More sophisticated programs offer desktop publishing facilities and other extras. With AmiPro (£99), for example, you can draw graphs to illustrate your business features with the latest data.

Word processing software packages are either DOS based or Windows based. DOS-based software tends to be quicker to use, but Windows-based software is easier to learn. Of the DOS word processing software, WordPerfect is the one most frequently used by editors. Among the Windows-based versions, AmiPro is the market leader, followed by Microsoft Word and WordPerfect for Windows.

Your software should have a spell-checker. The more vocabulary a spell-checker has, the faster it works, but the more mistakes it overlooks.

You can also buy additional grammar checker software (for example, Grammatik). This can pick up the grammatical slips you make when you write quickly.

There is also a good style checking program called StyleWriter, available for both Windows and DOS, which you can buy in addition to your word processing software. It picks up clichés, passive constructions, empty words, sexist phrases — in short, everything mentioned under 'Developing a good writing style' on page 77. It is slow to use, but you can speed it up by switching off certain functions. StyleWriter teachers you to write better, because it keeps pointing out over-long or passive sentences until you get so fed up that you stop using them. It also calculates the average sentence length of your articles, so you can compare it quickly with the average sentence length of your target publication.

Can I buy a second-hand computer?

Yes. You can get them from computer auctions, through adverts in the local newspaper, even at car boot sales. Second-hand computers are cheap, but not guaranteed. Many computer dealers stock second-hand computers, but you have to ask because they prefer selling you a new one. Dealers can check second-hand computers expertly and offer a warranty.

How can I get software cheaply?

Don't copy somebody else's software — it's illegal. You can buy second-hand software, but it is difficult to check that it is working well and there is always the risk of viruses. When buying second-hand software, make sure you get a legal, registered copy, complete with handbooks.

The cheapest way of getting new, good software is to buy old versions from the producers. Every software program is updated once a year or so, and the old versions are sold at a lower price. For example, you may get version 03 for £90, whereas version 04, which has a few minor extras, costs £350.

If you want to buy several programs — say, one for word processing, one for spreadsheets, one for accountancy and one for desktop publishing — you can often get amazing deals on packages.

Should I buy a desktop publishing program?

You don't need desktop publishing for journalism. However, many professional journalists do related work, for example edit corporate magazines and newsletters, using desktop publishing. The sample letters in this book were produced using PageMaker desktop publishing and the clipart library of CorelDraw.

How compatible are software programs?

Perhaps each of the publications for which you write uses a different system and different software. Is it possible to transfer information from one system to another?

Yes. Many of the bigger publishing houses have these facilities, or their typesetters or printers have them. However, it is not worth going through the process of transferring data this way for a single two-paragraph article.

Some editors ask for manuscripts in ASCII format. ASCII is the esperanto of the computer world. Imagine that your computer speaks one language, and your editor another, and they don't understand each other. But they both understand a third language, ASCII.

You write your articles as usual in your word processing software, but before you copy it onto a floppy disk for your editor you save it in ASCII format. Check with your software handbook if it is possible. Your editor's computer then translates the text from ASCII into the software used there.

Is it true that working at computers can affect the health?

Yes. Like almost every other type of work, computing can cause health problems, especially if you sit at your computer day after day, for hours on end.

Make sure that the keyboard and the screen are in an ideal position to avoid repetitive strain injury in the wrists, or stiff neck and shoulders. Select a comfortable, back-supporting chair with adjustable height. Prefer low radiation monitors. You can also buy anti-glare screens to cover your monitor. If sunlight falls in at an angle which makes it difficult to read the screen during certain times of the day, draw the curtains.

Try to break up your computer work for five minutes every hour. Make that essential phone call or get a cup of coffee. It's easy to get carried away when you are in the middle of a feature, and forget to take a break.

If your eyes get tired, your wrists or shoulders ache and you get a headache, take a break immediately. Either do writing-related work for which you don't need the computer (market study, filing) or go for a short walk.

13
Journalists Who've Made It
— and How

WHAT'S THEIR SECRET?

Freelance writers who make a living from writing articles and features reveal their secrets — including some of their most embarrassing moments!

John Dawes

Specialist subjects
Swimming pool technology and design; energy efficiency and conservation; author-publishing and production.

Membership
The Society of Authors; Scientific and Technical Authors Group within the Society of Authors; Small Press Group of GB; Author-Publisher Enterprise.

Recent publications
Includes features in *Professional Engineering; House Builder; Specification; New Scientist; Leisure Management; Licensee; Build-it; The Times.*

Books published
About ten non-fiction books.

First published article
'It was *Hobbies* magazine that attracted me to practical writing instead of arty-stuff production. The first published piece was Paired Coffee Tables . . . how to make them for less than 25 shillings, published in *Do It Yourself* 1961, a one-page how-to piece with detailed drawings and working sketches, no photos. Excellent position on the last page.'

Worst ever article
'That very first how-to article on paired coffee tables. It looked a practical, easy, clever how-to article. I can admit now that it was purely research-based, not practically seen through. I didn't make a coffee table until ten years later! My clever idea positioned three legs of each coffee table at the respective centres of gravity. Whoever made the tables this way would discover that they toppled over! This was before I discovered the value of a pen name. . .'

When did you feel you had made it?
'When my first book was published in 1975 by Bartholomew & Sons (the map people): a beautifully designed production titled *The Swimming Pool and the Garden.*'

When and why did you go freelance?
'This was when I changed my lifestyle from ''power complex company man'' to an individual in a small company business. I valued freedom of mind, action and work.'

Other writing related work
'As a confirmed author-publisher, I now self-publish most of my work since I have control over production, rights, sales and so on. Therefore I turn my hand to everything in the way of spreading information and ideas . . . a writing ''product processor''.'

Working time
Thirty hours per week research, ten hours per week writing, ten hours per week administration.

Equipment used
Electronic typewriter; AppleMac PC; basic wordprocessor, sophisticated software only for self-publishing needs; dot matrix and ink jet printers; phone; fax; modem; answerphone; recorder.

Greatest joy of being a freelance journalist
'Freedom of choice.'

Greatest frustrations of being a freelance journalist
'The non-productive bits; chasing for payment; spreading the load when working as an individual; getting started on the first blank sheet of paper in a project.'

Any ambitions left?
'Yes, many, but in the sphere of writing there is one major ambition not tackled yet . . . that is to do some ''real writing'' by producing a novel where the reader reads for pleasure, not profit. Non-fiction work is for necessity.'

Has the marked changed in recent years?
'Yes, the publishing scene is run generally by company men and women who put corporate politics before individual actions. Therefore, they seem no longer to be expressing freedom of mind.'

Advice to writers who want to break into print
'Have something you really want to say and know your subject inside and out.'

And to already successful writers planning to go full-time freelance
'Professionalise your activities. For example, use a pen name, use letterheads, offer a useful business card, sell your services at a high standard and high value.'

Is it worth specialising in a subject?
'Yes. Always make a subject or topic your own speciality to add value. The sooner the better, to be distinctive and competitive.'

Message to the readers of this book
'Independence of thought and action is essential for writers who wish to try to find and work ''original'' words. Discover and learn everything there is to absorb about the art and the craft of writing, as well as the processes of production and publication. Know your tools and technologies as well as your subject and idiosyncrasies.'

Jane Baker

Specialist subjects
None.

Membership
British Association of Industrial Editors.

Recent publications
Include features and articles in *Country Life, The Lady, Monocle* (a

Surrey glossy magazine), *Hospitality* (a catering trade magazine), *Home & Country* (WI magazine), *Company Digest*.

First published article

'I was a trainee reporter for four years, so my first story has rather been lost in time. However, two years ago I experienced a "first". I was very keen to get onto the news pages of *Country Life*, but was intimidated by the idea of approaching the news editor. She turned out to be charming, friendly and happy to consider my suggestions. I ended up becoming a regular contributor (with three changes of editor along the way). Because I overcame my fears I consider this one of my most satisfactory achievements.'

Worst ever article

'It must have been so bad that I've wiped it from my memory. But I remember an incident where I almost missed a good story because my journalistic antenna was switched off.

'One of my first interviews was with a couple celebrating their golden wedding anniversary. They were excessively boring and I was wondering what on earth I could write about them, when, poised on the doorstep about to depart, I asked if they had any other hobbies (we'd already covered gardening and so on). The wife shook her head, then added: "Well, I am a medium in my spare time". Luckily I was able to shuffle them back inside and get the details.

'Moral: dig around a bit and even the most boring facade can hide a fascinating interior.'

When did you feel you had made it?

'Writing my first review (for which I got a byline) for the local paper where I was apprenticed. It was a school's version of *Carmen* and gave me my first taste of writing personal opinions and in my own style. Heady stuff!'

When and why did you go freelance?

'In 1986. I was made redundant and decided to become a freelance which is something I had been considering for nearly a year.'

Other writing related work

Short stories, industrial editing, public relations, sales leaflets, manuscript assessments, tutoring in creative writing.

Equipment used
'Much-loved Amstrad 8256. It's really worth persevering with a PCW, they ease the burden of writing, storing, editing, etc.'

Working time
Six hours per week research, 20 hours writing, two hours admin.

Greatest joys of being a freelance journalist
'Being able to place features I've enjoyed writing. Being able to sneak free time when other people are working, even though it might mean working to midnight because I've spent a sunny afternoon in the garden.'

Greatest frustrations of being a freelance journalist
'Insecurity. Not being able to place what I think is a worthwhile feature. Not being able to break into some of the glossy consumer magazines. Having to gear myself up to try and "sell" myself and my material when I don't feel like it.'

Any ambitions left?
'To complete and publish a novel I am working on. To earn more money from fiction. To get into the glossy consumer mags. To be commissioned by the glossy consumer mags.'

Has the market changed in recent years?
'No, I don't think so. Editors are still looking for the same things: suitable stories, competently researched and written, on time, preferably illustrated.'

Advice to writers who want to break into print
'Study the market before approaching editors. Remember that you have to sell the idea of an article first. I spend a great deal of time on my query letter, or preparing to speak to an editor on the telephone, making sure I have the salient facts ready in their most attractive form.'

And to already successful writers planning to go full-time freelance
'Look carefully at whether you have the contacts, material and savings to make the leap. Do you have the right temperament to deal with the insecurity and the highs and lows?'

Is it worth specialising in a subject?
'I don't specialise. I'm a good all-rounder, although I try to write about

people within the arts and crafts field. I think it would have helped if I had specialised, and I would recommend that, once journalists have a good general founding, they choose a subject in which to become expert. This is because editors, especially those on national publications, seem to like to be able to grade you. They also know instantly who to call when subject comes up.'

Mike Gerrard

Specialised subjects
Computing, travel.

Membership
Writer's Guild; Society of Authors; British Guild of Travel Writers.

Recent publications
Include features (mostly about travel) in *The Guardian, The European, The Daily Telegraph, Washington Post, The Times.*

Books published
Six books on computing, several guidebooks on Yorkshire Dales, Greece and Corfu.

First published article
'When I was in my teens, an article on Lancashire music which earned me ten guineas, in *Lancashire Life*. I had a bit of expertise because I collected folk music.'

Worst ever article
'I don't remember my worst stories, but they must have been among those rejected by *Mayfair*. I sent them a story about being discovered with the head girl in a cupboard at a Catholic training college, which they accepted immediately and paid well. I thought that's easy money, so I sent them a lot of stuff, all of which was returned. Some of these stories must have been dreadful. After a while I realised that *Mayfair* wasn't such an easy market after all.'

When did you feel you made it?
'It happened gradually.'

When and why did you go freelance?
'I always wanted to be a writer, but I thought I would write television

comedies. It never occurred to me that I would be a freelance journalist. I worked in accountancy, then did a teacher training course. I realised that neither was the right career for me, and gave up teacher training to go freelance. Luckily, I had the big break-through just the week after I took the decision.

'While I was studying at teacher training college, I did a correspondence course in writing. I know these courses don't work for everyone, but they worked for me. After a few months I had earned my course fee back by selling articles. I also did casual work in hotels, and worked for a literary agent in London. The latter was valued experience.'

Other writing related work
Photography, teaching journalism (especially travel journalism).

Equipment used
A personal computer.

Working time
'On average, one week per month on research (travelling). When I'm back at my desk, I write from 8am to about 11am, then I rewrite and edit what I've written. I spend the rest of the day on administration (like in any other business) and sending out query letters.'

Greatest joys of being a freelance journalist
'The feeling of independence. The freedom to take a day off without having to ask permission. Of course you work long hours if you are self-employed, but you can juggle your time to suit you. I would never go back to employed work for someone else, unless forced.'

Greatest frustrations of being a freelance journalist?
'The worst bit is the uncertainty of income. This is difficult; it is a permanent feature of freelance life. It is either feast or famine. You don't get your money regularly; publishers pay when they choose to publish. Sometimes, when the income drops, I wake up at night and worry. After 15 years of successful freelancing I still have those periods when I'm worrying. But if nobody commissions work, I send out lots of query letters with ideas, which leads to work and income.'

Any ambitions left?
'I still want to be a television comedy writer.'

Has the market changed in recent years?
'Yes, it has become harder. The market has contracted with the recession, and of course there are more people (including redundant staff
journalists) competing for less space. I know quite a few people who
had to give up. Having said that, I have observed that the situation has
been getting a bit better recently.'

Advice to writers who want to break into print
'The main thing is determination. You must feel that you're going to get
there: the people who succeed are those who have this determination.'

And to already successful writers planning to go full-time freelance
'You need a constant source of ideas. In fact, you are the editors' source
of ideas — they rely on you to come up with new suggestions.
    'For travel articles, eavesdrop on people's conversations; you can get
the most amazing quotes. Give your travel articles a bold, surprising, if
possible funny beginning.'

Is it worth specialising in a subject?
'Yes. I specialised first in computers, and now in travel writing.'

Message to the readers of this book
'Travel writing is a competitive market, but there is no barrier to it. The
market is open to everyone.'

Christine Hall

Specialist subjects
International employment and career topics, education, languages, publishing, small businesses, international business, Germany, China,
travel, oriental dancing.

Membership
Society of Women Writers and Journalists; Society of Authors; International PEN; Women Writers' Network; Federation of Kent Writers.

Recent publications
Include features in *Company Magazine, Overseas Jobs Express, Jobs
International, Quartos, Escape — The Career Change Magazine, Lan-
guage Travel Gazette, Südkurier* (Germany), *Your Business, Habibi*
(USA), *The English Coaching Paper* (China), *Acclaim, Great Ideas,
Freelance Writing & Photography, Business Opportunities World,*

Freelance Writing & Photography, The Lady, Woman Alive, Der Spiegel (Germany).

Books published
How to Get a Job in Germany; How to Be a Freelance Journalist; How to Live and Work in Germany; Living & Working in China (forthcoming).

First published article
'I had an eye injury and could not get treatment because none of the eye specialists in the area was available. Half of them were on holiday, the others at a congress for eye specialists! I was so furious that I wrote an article and posted it to the free local paper. They put it in a big, bold frame on page 3, with byline. It was the talk of the town.'

Worst ever article
'I interviewed a local vet who claimed she had just performed the first-ever cancer operation on a rat in central Europe. She boasted what a difficult job she had done. She said rats were such unusual pets and nobody knew how to anaesthetise them. I interviewed the owner (who was a friend of mine) to add human interest, and I photographed the rat which still seemed dizzy and afraid of the flash.

'The editor of the local paper loved the piece. I was proud to see it in print, under the headline Operation Succeeded — Patient Survived — until I heard my sister-in-law, a scientist in pharmaceutical research, complain: "What a load of rubbish they are printing in the paper nowadays. What kind of vet is this who doesn't know how to anaesthetise a rat? No animal is anaesthetised more frequently..."

'Luckily the article did not carry my byline.

'To make things worse, the rat had died before the article was printed, and the owner blamed the flash of my camera. She did not talk to me for weeks!

'But the newspaper readers queued outside the vet's surgery. They all wanted their hamsters and budgies treated by the miracle vet who had, overnight, become a local celebrity...'

When did you feel you had made it?
'When editors phoned to ask me for features instead of me begging them to look at my work. (I'll know that I've achieved VIP writer status when people start claiming that Christine Hall's books were not written by Christine Hall. This would put me in the same category as Homer, Shakespeare, Margaret Mitchell, Shirley Conran and Jeffrey Archer.)'

When and why did you go freelance?
'When I returned from China I decided that I preferred being independent and my own boss. Instead of hunting for a job in London, I settled down in the countryside, starting up my own editorial business. By that time I had developed several good markets and my name was known to editors in my subject areas.

'I had worked in publishing and editing for over ten years, as trainee publisher, subeditor, production editor, features editor, copy editor, deputy editor and acting editor. This inside knowledge helped a lot. I was nervous when I took the plunge — everyone who starts up a business is — but I was also confident that I could make it.'

Other writing related work
Freelance editing (for example brochures and newsletters, or standing in for magazine newspaper editorial staff who are on holiday or sick); consultancy and criticism service (features, short stories and non-fiction books only); giving talks, lectures and workshops and teaching journalism at courses.

Equipment used
A personal computer (BDS) for word processing (WordPerfect for DOS, AmiPro for Windows), style checking (StyleWriter), graphic design (CorelDraw) and desktop publishing (PageMaker), as well as clipart libraries for editing newsletters and brochures. A dot matrix printer (Epson LX400) for manuscripts and a laser printer (Panasonic KX-P4410) for correspondence and camera ready copy. A combined telephone/answering machine/telefax (BT DF200) which is worth its weight in gold (excuse the cliché). Three cameras (including a second-hand autofocus, Olympus) one for print film, one for slides and one for b/w.

Working time
Ten hours per week research, 20 hours writing, ten hours administration.

Greatest joys of being a freelance journalist
'Developing new ideas; interviewing people; constantly learning about new things; seeing my work in print; being invited as a speaker to writers' groups and courses; being my own boss; being able to go for a walk on a sunny morning and work at night instead.'

Greatest frustrations of being a freelance journalist
'The unproductive administration work, especially book-keeping and

filing (I'm now employing a book-keeper who does in two hours what used to take me two days); aching wrists after six hours at the keyboard; people who think that writing isn't real work.'

Any ambitions left?
'Being headhunted as launch editor of a national magazine; being invited on press trips to write about exotic places to which I could not otherwise afford to travel for research; receiving an honorary doctorate of a university when I'm old and wise; contributing regularly to the daily newspapers; earning enough to employ a full-time housekeeper who does all the cleaning, washing-up and ironing which I hate!'

Has the market changed in recent years?
'Yes, it is more competitive; subjects in demand are more money and sex-oriented.'

Advice to writers who want to break into print
'Study one or two potential markets in depth and write articles specifically for them. Join a good writers' group, and subscribe to at least one writing magazine for a year. Put a lot of enthusiasm and time into your writing.'

And to already successful writers planning to go full-time
'Regard it as a proper business. Develop marketing skills. Like every self-employed person, you must learn to sell your goods.'

Is it worth specialising in a subject?
'Definitely. This is the only way to keep your research time to a realistic minimum, and to become known as an expert journalist.'

Message to the readers of this book
'Journalism is one of the most rewarding careers, but you will only succeed if you are prepared to work hard.'

Glossary

Article
A piece of journalistic writing, usually short and topical.

Boxed item
A piece of factual information (contacts, phone numbers, figures) added to a feature, often printed in a frame.

Bullet
The dots at the beginning of paragraphs. Often used as a design element in magazines, for example in how-to articles. Journalists indicate bullets with asterisks in their manuscripts.

Byline
A published line identifying the writer, for example 'By Cathy Clever'.

Caption
The text which explains the contents of a picture.

Commissioned
Articles written 'to order' for an editor who gives detailed instructions and promises to buy the completed work at an agreed price.

Copy
Journalistic jargon for text.

Deadline
The date by which you must submit the finished article of feature.

DTP; desktop publishing
Computer programs used by most publishing houses to design and make up pages on screen, instead of the traditional method of pasting paper on cardboard. PageMaker and Quark Xpress are popular with publishers.

Expenses

The money you spend to research and write your article, for example train tickets to meet an interviewee. Some (but not all) editors pay expenses on top of the rate if the work is commissioned.

Feature

A piece of journalistic writing which deals with a subject in depth, not necessarily topical, but usually longer than an article. There is no strict division between articles and features. For some newspapers, every piece of more than 250 words is a 'feature'. Others draw the dividing line between 'article' and 'feature' at 2500 words.

Freebie

Samples of products or services given to journalists to try out free, to encourage reviews.

House style

A sheet for staff and freelance writers with information about which words, spellings and so on the publication prefers.

Intro

The first paragraph of a journalistic piece, often printed in bigger or bolder typeface than the rest. Must capture the reader.

Ms; Manuscript

The typewritten text you submit to the editor.

On spec

On speculation. Sending a manuscript to an editor without guarantee that it will be bought.

Proof

Print out of the typeset work. Usually checked (proofread) by subeditors or proofreaders.

Sae; Stamped, addressed envelope

Must be enclosed with every manuscript submission (except commissioned work, or features which the editor has asked to see). Large enough, and with sufficient postage, for the return of your work.

Story

Journalistic jargon for feature or article. Don't confuse with the fictional short story.

Syndication

Selling the same article or feature several times, to non-competing publications, for example to magazines in different countries.

Further Reading

BOOKS

Writing for Newspapers, Jill Dick (A & C Black, £9.99). Useful for writers who want to specialise in newspaper journalism. With detailed sections on editorial production and writing style, as well as addresses of newspapers and tips on how to submit urgent commissioned copy over the phone.

Writing for Magazines, Jill Dick (A & C Black, £9.99). Covers ideas, market research, tailoring ideas to different magazines, style and structure, selling work, interviewing, supplying pictures and problem solving.

Research for Writers, Ann Hoffmann (A & C Black, £10.99). Useful for writers who need to research their specialist subjects in depth. Contains advice on copyright, on how to trace periodicals, how to get information from foreign countries, and plenty of addresses of archives, public record offices and so on.

How to Write for Publication, Chriss McCallum (How To Books, £8.99). This book is packed with advice on all aspects of freelance writing, from query letters to short story competitions, manuscript layout, agents and the law of libel. It contains a surprising amount of comprehensive information for a compact book format, and is clearly structured. Warmly recommended to beginners, as well as to professional journalists who want to explore other areas of writing.

Write and Get Paid for It, Terry Prone (Poolbeg). This is another comprehensive source of writing advice for authors and journalists at all levels. Written in an entertaining style, with lots of anecdotes and 'true stories' from the author's experience.

How to Sell and Re-sell Your Writing, Duane Newcomb (Writers Digest). Deals with getting ideas and marketing your work. Practical suggestions on how to sell each article several times. The only drawback is that all examples refer to American markets, and some of the magazines mentioned have ceased publication.

Make Every Word Count, Gary Provost (Writers Digest). This book offers far more than the usual boring repetition of basic grammar. It gives real advice on how to sharpen your writing style. Writers at all levels find advice on how to give their style more life, spirit, flourish and pace, how to avoid redundant words and how to use associations. Subeditors will cherish your style.

Writing Feature Articles, Brendan Hennessy (Heinemann Professional Publishing). A practical book with detailed advice on many subjects, from organising your time to reviewing books, and a funny section on techniques for tough interview questions.

Writers' & Artists' Yearbook (A & C Black, £9.99). The front section contains addresses, for example publications in the UK and abroad, complete with frequency, editor's name, address, telephone number, retail price, and often the rates of pay and the type of work requested. The addresses of syndication agents are valuable for professional journalists. The second half contains information on copyright and libel, income tax and allowances, societies and prizes, as well as the standard correction marks and how to use them. The book is updated every year.

Successful Article Writing, Gillian Thornton (Writers News, £10.95). Practical book for beginners, includes sections on humour and on writing about pets.

If you find it difficult to obtain books about writing, you can subscribe to a book club which specialises in books for writers and journalists: Writers Bookshop, Writers News Ltd, PO Box 4, Nairn IV12 4HU.

BOOKLETS AND BROCHURES

Directory of Writers' Circles, now in its seventh edition. £4 post free from Jill Dick, Oldacre, Horderns Park Road, Chapel en le Frith, Derbyshire SK12 6SY.

Directory of Postal Workshops, £1.50 from Catherine Gill, Drakemyre Croft, Cairnorrie, Methlick, Ellon, Aberdeenshire AB41 0JN.

The Society of Authors offers a series of information booklets and quick guides for writers. Of particular interest to journalists are: *Copyright* (£1), *Libel* (£1), *The Small Claims Court* (£1), *Buying a Word Processor* (£1), *Income Tax* (£1), *VAT* (£1), *Sell Your Writing* (£3). Send a cheque to: Publications Department, The Society of Authors, 84 Drayton Gardens, London SW10 9SB.

Travel Writing by Mike Gerrard contains sample articles, tips on how to research and write up your features, and an interview with a travel editor.

£1.50: Mike Gerrard, 5 Parsonage Street, Wistow, Huntingdon, Cambridgeshire PE17 2QD.

Keeping Records and Accounts, VAT Cash Accounting, Should I be Registered for VAT? The VAT Guide, all written in plain English and available free from your local VAT office (you find the address in your phone book under Customs and Excise).

MAGAZINES

Active Life, ASM, Christchurch, Cosway Street, London SW1 5NS.

Chat, IPC Magazines, King's Reach Tower, Stamford Street, London SE1 9LS.

Company, National Magazine House, 72 Broadwick Street, London W1V 2BP.

The Disabled Driver, Cottingham Way, Thrapston, Kettering NN14 4PL.

European Frozen Food Buyer and *European Drinks Buyer,* Crier Publications, Arctic House, Rye Lane, Dunton Green, Sevenoaks, Kent TN14 5HB.

Good Housekeeping, 72 Broadwick St, London W1V 2BP.

Great Ideas, Business Innovations Research, Tregeraint House, Zennor, St Ives, Cornwall TR26 3DB.

Here's Health, Victory House, 14 Leicester Place, London WC2H 7BP.

The Kent & Sussex Courier, Longfield Road, Tunbridge Wells TN2 3HL.

PC Magazine, Cottons Centre, Hay's Lane, London SE1 2QT.

Popular Crafts Magazine, Argus House, Boundary Way, Hemel Hempstead, Herts HP2 7ST.

Practical Fishkeeping and *Fishkeeping Answers,* Bretton Court, Bretton, Peterborough PE3 8DZ.

The Stage and Television Today, 47 Bermondsey St, London SE1 3XT.

Quartos Magazine, BCM-Writer, 27 Old Gloucester Street, London WC1N 3XX.

Stamp Lover, National Philatelic Society, 107 Charterhouse Street, London EC1M 6PT.

Stationery Trade News, Trace Media Limited, Brookmead House, Two Rivers, Station Lane, Witney, Oxon OX8 6BH.

Steam Classic, Ebony, Heathlands Industrial Estate, Heathlands Road, Liskeard, Cornwall PL14 4HD.

UK Press Gazette, Maclean Hunter House, Chalk Lane, Cockfosters Road, Barnet, Herts EN4 0BU.

Writers News, PO Box 4, Nairn IV12 4HU.

What Personal Computer, 33-39 Bowling Green Lane, London EC1R 0DA.

Woman, IPC Magazines, King's Reach Tower, Stamford St, London SE1 9LS.

Useful Addresses

COURSES

Please enclose sae with your enquiry.

Arvon Foundation, Totleigh Barton, Sheepwash, Beaworthy, Devon EX21
5NS. Tel: (01422) 843714.

Belstead House, Belstead, Ipswich IP8 3NA. Tel: (01473) 686321. Fax:
(01473) 686664.

Dillington House, Ilminster, Somerset TA19 9DT. Tel: (01460) 52427.
Fax: (01460) 52433.

East Midlands Arts' Residential Writing Retreats, The Arts Training Pro-
gramme, De Montfort University, Scraptoft Campus, Leicester LE7
9SU.

Fen Farm, 1 Angel Hill, Bury St Edmunds, Suffolk IP33 1UZ. Tel: (01284)
753110.

Flair For Words, 5 Delavall Walk, Eastbourne BN23 6ER. Tel: (01323)
640646.

The London School of Journalism, 1-4 Daniel Mews, Bathwick, Bath. Tel:
(01225) 444774. Fax: (01225) 313986.

Millers House Hotel, Middleham, Wensleydale, North Yorkshire DL8
4NR. Tel: (01969) 22630. Fax: (01969) 22630.

National Council for the Training of Journalists, Latton Bush Centre,
Southern Way, Harlow, Essex CM18 7BI. Tel: (01279) 430009.

PMA Training, The Old Anchor, Church Street, Hemingford Grey, Cambs
PE18 9DF. Tel: (01480) 300653. Fax: (01480) 496022.

Taliesin Trust, Ty Newydd, Llanystumdwy, Cricieth, Gwynedd LL52 0LW.
Tel: (01766) 522811. Fax: (01766) 523095.

The Writers Bureau Ltd, Sevendale House, 7 Dale Street, Manchester M1
1JB. Tel: (0161) 228 2362.

Writers' News Home Study Division, PO Box 4, Nairn IV12 4HU.

The Writers' Summer School, Philippa Boland, The Red House, Mardens
Hill, Crowborough, East Sussex TN8 1XN. Tel: (01892) 653943.

CRITICISM AND ADVISORY SERVICES

Please enclose sae with your enquiry.

Jane Baker, 6 Bramble Way, Send Marsh, Ripley, Surrey GU22 6LL. Tel: (01483) 223860.

Flair For Words, 5 Delavall Walk, Eastbourne BN23 6ER. Tel: (01323) 640646.

Dr Hilary Johnson, 5 St Agnes Gate, Wendover, Bucks MP22 6DP. Tel: (01296) 623260.

Scriptease Editorial, Christine Hall, Finchden, Sandhurst, Cranbrook, Kent TN18 5JS. Tel/fax: (01580) 850687.

ORGANISATIONS

Please enclose sae with your enquiry.

Arts Council of Great Britain, 14 Great Peter Street, London SW1P 3NQ. Tel: (0171) 333 0100.

Author-Publisher Enterprise, John Dawes, 12 Mercers, Hawkhurst, Kent TN18 4LH. Tel: (01580) 753346.

The British Guild of Travel Writers, c/o Paul Mansfield, Membership Secretary, 36 Sanford Road, Brighton, East Sussex BN1 5DJ.

International PEN, 7 Dilke Street, Chelsea, London SW3 4JE. Tel: (0171) 352 6303. Fax: (0171) 351 0220.

National Council for the Training of Journalists, Latton Bush Centre, Southern Way, Harlow, Essex CM18 7BI. Tel: (01279) 430009.

The Society of Authors, 84 Drayton Gardens, London SW10 9SB. Tel: (0171) 373 6642. Fax: (0171) 373 5768.

The Society of Freelance Editors and Proofreaders, 38 Rochester Road, London NW1 9GG.

The Society of Women Writers & Journalists, c/o Geraldine Beare, Membership Secretary, 39 Victoria Rd, Knaphill, Woking, Surrey GU21 2AU.

Women Writers Network, c/o Cathy Smith, Membership Secretary, 23 Prospect Road, London NW2 2JU.

Index